COMPUTER OLYMPICS

STEPHEN MANES AND PAUL SOMERSON

A HARD/SOFT PRESS BOOK

SCHOLASTIC INC.
New York Toronto London Auckland Sydney Tokyo

ISBN 0-590-33176-0

Copyright © 1984 by Hard/Soft Inc. All rights reserved. Published by Scholastic Inc.

Program adaptations by McMullen & McMullen, Inc.

Designed by Gene Siegel

12 11 10 9 8 7 6 5 4 3   8/8

Printed in U.S.A.   34

To Jean, paragon of patience

Welcome, Olympian!

Would you like to win an Olympic gold medal?

Have you ever dreamed of running the marathon or entering the decathlon?

Do you have what it takes to be a world-famous basketball hero?

Can you light the Olympic torch?

With this book and your home computer you'll be able to do all these things — and a whole lot more!

Just be sure to read our GOLD MEDAL TIPS AND TRICKS before you begin!

GOLD MEDAL TIPS AND TRICKS: The Olympic programmers answer your questions

You may be tempted to skip this section and go right on to the programs. You know what we say to that? **DON'T!!!!**
Running BASIC programs is fun. So is typing them in. But there are times when programming can make *you* throw in the towel. In this section, we'll give you lots of tips to help you keep going for the gold.

Will these programs run on my computer?

If you have an IBM Personal Computer or IBM PCjr, the answer is YES! All you have to do is type in the Program Listing. You shouldn't need to make any changes at all.

If you have any of the following computers, the answer is still YES!

> Apple II
> Apple II Plus
> Apple IIe
> Atari 400, 800 or XL Series
> Coleco ADAM
> Commodore 64 or VIC-20
> Radio Shack TRS-80 Color Computer
> Texas Instruments 99/4A

With these computers, you'll usually have to change the Program Listing slightly. Most of the time only a line or two will be different.

Just be sure to read the "If You Have . . ." section that appears after every Program Listing. It always tells you *exactly* what changes you'll need to make for your computer. (The ADAM needs special changes. Keep reading to learn how to make them.)

It's a good idea to read the "If You Have . . ." information *before* you start typing in your program. If this is your own copy of *Computer Olympics,* you may want to use a pen or pencil to mark the Program Listing with the changes you'll need.

There's more information about each of these computers at the end of this section. Be sure to read it before starting out!

If you have any other computer, the answer is still YES! But you may have to experiment until you find the exact changes your machine needs to run each program. That should be simple. We've tried hard to use only the parts of BASIC that are available on most machines.

Will my program run as soon as I type it in?

If a program runs as soon as you type it in, you're an absolutely amazing typist — and a very lucky one! Everybody makes little typing mistakes — even us experts! But in a computer program, little mistakes can cause BIG trouble.

If a program doesn't seem to run right, or if you get an error message — something like "Syntax Error" or "SN?" or "You Dummy!" — you'll have to go hunting for your mistakes. Programmers call them bugs. Remember, you put them there, and your program won't run right until you squish out every last one! The official word for that is "debugging."

How do I get the bugs out of my program?

When you type in a program, you must type each line exactly as it appears in the listing. If you miss even one space or one comma, your program probably won't run the way it should.

First, check your program line by line against the listing in the book. It's a good idea to LIST only a few lines at a time, using commands like LIST 100–150. That way, the whole LIST won't scroll up your screen before you get a chance to read it.

You'll probably slap your head when you discover the idiotic goofs you made. With some computers, you'll have to type the whole line in again to make a correction. With others, you can just type in the changes. Learn which way your computer works: It'll save you lots of typing.

Second, be sure you've made the changes your particular machine needs. *Always* look at the "If You Have . . ." section for your particular computer.

2

If your program still doesn't run, don't give up! There are plenty of things you may have done wrong. How do we know? Because we do them all the time ourselves! Here are some things to watch out for:

Rotten Leftovers

When you start typing in a program, be sure to type NEW and hit the ENTER (or RETURN) key. If you don't, you may find leftover lines from an old program popping up in your new one. It can be a real mess to get them out!

The Curse of the Missing Line Number

It's easy to skip a line by accident when you're typing a long program. Remember: Every program in this book includes a REM statement on line 10 with the name of the program. The next line in every program is line 100, and the lines count up by tens from there, like this:

```
10 REM USELESS PROGRAM
100 INPUT X
110 INPUT Y
120 PRINT Z
```

The only line numbers that won't end in 0 will be lines you add from the "If You Have . . ." section. And the only time the lines will skip — say from 240 to 260 — is when the "If You Have . . ." section tells you to remove a line for your machine.

One Out of Two

Some things have to come in pairs, or your computer will get terribly upset. What kinds of things? Mainly quotation marks ("") and left and right parentheses (()). Leaving one out is just about guaranteed to get you some sort of error message. That's why it's important to check a statement like

```
300 PRINT CHR$(INT(RND(1)*(3+2)/(4+3)))
```

very carefully. If you're not positive, count the parentheses and quotation marks on your *other* personal computer — your fingers!

A Letter's Not a Number

Your computer is very, very fussy about letters and numbers. Remember, a one (1) is not a small L (l) or a capital i (I), even though they may look almost the same. And as far as the computer is concerned, a capital letter o (O) is not the same as the number zero (∅).

In our Program Listings, you'll always find a slash through the number zero (∅) to keep you from getting confused. But your fingers may do something your brain never had in mind!

Here are some program lines that will cause your computer to scratch its head and give up. We stole them from our own wastebaskets. Each line contains just one error. Can you spot the goofs?

```
100  GOT∅ 240
200  1F I=2 THEN 500
300  N=J
400  R=22I
500  P=4I6
```

A Space Isn't Nothing!

Especially in graphics programs — programs that draw pictures — spaces are terribly important. If the Program Listing shows a space, be sure you don't leave it out. For example, in

```
100  F$="MURBLEHEAD"
110  PRINT F$;" IS A JERK!"
```

if you leave out the space between the first quotation mark and the word IS in line 11∅, you'll get this:

```
MURBLEHEADIS A JERK!
```

You can probably guess what prints out if you leave the space in.

But don't add spaces where there are none in the listing. That may cause problems that are even worse!

Semicolons and Commas

Semicolons and commas have special jobs in BASIC programs. Semicolons let you PRINT more than one thing on each line. In PRINT statements, commas do the same thing a little differently, but the programs in this book hardly ever use them that way.

In DATA statements, commas separate each item of data. If you leave one out or put an extra one in, it will confuse your computer. If you get a message like "Out of Data" when everything in your program looks right, chances are you left out a comma — or perhaps a whole DATA statement.

Mysterious Letters

Sometimes the letters and names used for variables in a program can get confusing. It's easy to type an E when you meant to type a D. They're right next to each other on the keyboard. So watch out! One mistake like that can keep an almost perfect program from running at all.

A Real Live Bug?

If you've done everything you can think of, and you're positive we've missed a bug in our own program, please write and describe the problem. We'll try to come up with a solution!

Why did you include the Sample Runs?

The Sample Runs are here for two reasons. First, they give you an idea of what the programs will do. That way, you can decide whether or not you want to type in a particular program.

The Sample Runs are also here to help you make sure your program is running the way it should. But remember: There are some things you can do on a computer that you can't do on a printed page. Many of these programs create pictures that move across your screen. There's no way we can show that here.

And some of the programs do different things every time you run them. So when you run your program, it may not do *exactly* what the Sample Run does — but it should come close.

How come the program listings are in ALL CAPITALS?

If you've already peeked at the Program Listings, you'll notice they're entirely in capital letters. That's because some computers only have capitals. If your machine is one of them, you won't have any problems with any of these programs.

But if you've got a computer that can give you both capitals *and* lower-case letters, you may run into some problems when you RUN these programs. Why? Let's say we ask a question that has a yes or no answer. You type in "yes" — all lowercase. But the program will be looking for "YES" — all capitals.

The solution? It's easy. Just press the key called CAPS LOCK or ALPHA LOCK or just plain LOCK on your computer. Do it when you type in your programs and when you run them. That way, all the letters will appear in CAPITALS!

What's an ENTER key? My computer doesn't have one!

One of the strangest and most important keys on the keyboard is the one you use to INPUT data. The strange part is that computer companies can't agree on what to call it. Some call it the ENTER key. Some call it the RETURN key. And some put a weird symbol on it and no lettering at all!

It's always in roughly the same place — to the right of the letters on the keyboard. Our Program Listings always call it the ENTER key. If you've got a RETURN key, you'll need to type that word into your PRINT statements wherever we've used the word ENTER.

That brings up another rule we've used in this book. Whenever a program asks you to answer a question or make a choice, you have to hit the ENTER (or RETURN) key before anything will happen. That means you can use the BACKSPACE key to correct any mistakes before you ENTER your answer into the computer.

If you're a good programmer, you'll also notice that we've tried hard to keep you from entering an answer the computer isn't expecting. If we ask for a number between 1 and 4, you won't be able to enter 5 — or 0!

My machine doesn't have a BREAK key. Or does it?

The BREAK key is something else that's different on every machine. Sometimes it's just a key marked BREAK. Sometimes it's really two keys — CTRL and BREAK or some other combination that you have to hold down at the same time. We'll tell you exactly which combination works for your computer in a second. Be sure you know how to use it!

Why? Well, some of our programs will run forever unless you BREAK out of them — or turn off your machine! Sometimes a typing error will make the same thing happen when it's not supposed to. And when you're debugging a program, you may only want to run a small part of it and then quit. It's the same with computers as it is with cars — knowing how to get your machine to stop when you want it to is a really lucky BREAK.

How can I keep my programs from disappearing when I turn off the computer?

Many of the programs in this book will take you only a few minutes to type in. The long ones may take a few hours. And once you turn your computer off, all your hard work will disappear.

But if you have a cassette recorder or disk drive, you can SAVE your programs and RUN them again and again. SAVEs are different on almost every machine. The instruction manual that came with your computer or disk drive should tell you how to SAVE your work — and LOAD it back into your computer again.

You don't have to wait until a program is working to SAVE it. Especially with longer programs, you should SAVE now and then as you type the program in. That way, you'll be able to LOAD everything you've done right back into your machine if your dog or cat or little sister accidentally pulls the plug — or if you've had enough of programming for one day and decide to go to the movies.

If you've got a friend with the same kind of computer as yours, you can each type in different programs and SAVE them on disk or cassette. Then you can swap your disks or cassettes. It's another great way to save yourself some typing!

I've got a printer. What about me?

You're really in luck! With a little thought, you'll be able to print out your very own personalized program runs. Do computer-makers agree on the way to get information to your printer? Not any more than they agree on the name of the ENTER (RETURN?) key!

With some machines, it's easy to print out your program runs. All you do is type something like PR#1, and everything you see on the screen will magically turn up on your printer, too!

With other machines it's a little trickier. You may have to change PRINT statements to LPRINT to get your printer to notice them. The best advice we can give is to check the manuals for your computer.

But remember this: If you try to run a program and absolutely *nothing* happens, it's a good bet that you tried to send something to your printer — and your printer wasn't turned on! On most machines, that's an excellent way to stop a program cold!

I can think of a better way to do some of the things you did. Why did you do them your way?

There are usually lots of different ways to get your computer to do the same thing. If you run this program:

```
10 PRINT "JESKLER LOVES PRUNES"
20 PRINT "JESKLER LOVES PRUNES"
```

you'll get exactly the same result as:

```
10 FOR A=1 TO 2
20 PRINT "JESKLER LOVES PRUNES"
30 NEXT A
```

We can think of at least ten other ways to get the same two lines printed out on the screen.

Which way is best? It all depends. If we've done something that looks silly to you, it may be because we've tried to get it to work with machines that can't do some things yours can.

We've tried to write our programs so they'll run on as many machines as possible. If we've left out your favorite BASIC command or done something in a roundabout way, we apologize. But if we've done something *really* stupid, let us know about it!

Will I mess up my computer if I make changes in your programs?

No! In fact, we *hope* you'll try to improve on these programs — and use them as a starting point for your own. But it's probably a good idea to get them running in their original versions first.

How do I run a program once I've typed it in?

Just type RUN and hit the ENTER or RETURN key!

What else do I have to read in this chapter?

Just the section on your own computer. After that — happy programming!

What if I have an IBM Personal Computer or PCjr?

You're in luck! These programs will run on your machine without any changes at all!

You should be sure to start off in BASIC by typing the command KEY OFF (and hitting the ENTER key). If you have a color monitor or TV set, you should next type WIDTH 40 (and the ENTER key again). You can choose the colors that you see on the screen by giving COLOR commands before you begin — or by writing them into the beginning of the program. The manual that comes with your computer will give you the details.

Remember to set the CAPS LOCK key so that you only get CAPITAL letters. To BREAK out of a program on a PC, hold down the CTRL key and press the BREAK key (it's also called SCROLL LOCK). To BREAK out on a PCjr, press the Fn key and then the letter B (for break). The PC's ENTER key has no lettering on it — just a funny arrow with a bent tail.

What if I have an Apple II Computer?

Many of these programs will run on your machine without any changes at all. In some programs, you'll have to remove one RANDOMIZE statement and change the way the program clears the screen. The "If You Have . . ." section after each Program Listing will tell you exactly what to do.

Be sure you run these programs in Applesoft BASIC — Apple's Integer BASIC just won't work. When you need to BREAK out of a program, hold down the CONTROL key and press the letter C. Your machine has a RETURN key instead of an ENTER key. If you have an Apple IIe, you should set the CAPS LOCK key so that you only get CAPITAL letters.

What if I have an Atari Computer?

Atari BASIC is very unusual. It doesn't allow string arrays like N$(3). It makes you DIMension all your string variables before you can use them. It requires a special way of entering string commands. It lacks features such as the TAB function.

Most of these programs will need simple changes and additions. The "If You Have . . ." section after each Program Listing will tell you exactly what to do.

Your machine has a BREAK key to let you break out of a program. It has a RETURN key instead of an ENTER key. And you can change the colors that appear on your screen—check your manual for the details.

What if I have a Coleco ADAM?

Many of these programs will run on your machine without any changes at all. In some programs, you'll have to remove one RANDOMIZE statement and change the way the program clears the screen. Because the version of BASIC in ADAM is almost exactly like the one for the Apple, you'll usually be able to follow the directions for Apple computers in the "If You Have . . ." section after each Program Listing.

But since the ADAM does not display as many characters across the screen as Apples do, you will have to make changes to some programs—especially the ones that make pictures. The following steps will help you get the programs running on your ADAM:

1. Enter the program, making the changes needed for the Apple Computer.
2. Now look at the changes for the TRS-80 Color Computer. *Don't* change any of the lines you already changed for the Apple. *Don't* change any lines that include the words CLS, LINE INPUT, RND or SOUND. Make all other changes needed for the Color Computer.

When you need to BREAK out of a program, hold down the CONTROL key and press the letter C. Your machine has a RETURN key instead of an ENTER key. And you should set the LOCK key so that you only get CAPITAL letters.

What if I have a Commodore 64 or VIC-20?

Many of these programs will run on your machine without any changes at all. In some programs, you'll have to remove a RANDOMIZE statement. In some, you'll also need to change one number in RND statements and change the way the program clears the screen. The "If You Have . . ." section after each Program Listing will tell you exactly what to do.

Your machine has a RETURN key instead of an ENTER key. To BREAK out of a program, press the RUN/STOP key. You may want to change the colors that appear on your screen. Your computer's manual will tell you exactly how to do it.

Since the VIC prints fewer characters (letters and numbers) on the screen than most other home computers, you may want to adjust the PRINT statements so that words don't "wrap" around the ends of lines. The easiest way is to divide one PRINT statement into two. If you do this, be sure the first PRINT statement keeps its original line number.

What if I have a Texas Instruments 99/4A Computer?

TI BASIC is unusual in many ways. It uses special characters instead of AND and OR. It uses the term SEG$ instead of the more common MID$. It's very fussy about what you can put after the word THEN.

Most of these programs will need simple changes and additions. The "If You Have . . ." section after each Program Listing will tell you exactly what to do.

Your machine has an ENTER key. To BREAK out of a program, hold down the FCTN key and press the number 4 key. You should set the ALPHA LOCK key so that you only get CAPITAL letters. You may want to change the colors that appear on your screen. Your computer's manual will tell you how to do it.

What if I have a TRS-80 Color Computer?

Many of these programs will run on your machine without any changes at all. In some, you'll have to take out one RANDOMIZE statement and change the way RND works. The "If You Have . . ." section after each Program Listing will tell you exactly what to do.

Your machine has an ENTER key and a BREAK key. You may want to change the colors that appear on your screen. Your computer's manual will tell you how to do it.

NOW, ON TO THE FUN!

Carry the Torch

The Olympic torch will go halfway around the world in its journey from Greece to Los Angeles. Now you can carry that torch right to your computer screen!

☐ Sample Run

```
YOU'VE CARRIED THE OLYMPIC FLAME
DOWN THE FINAL STRETCH TO THE
STADIUM.  NOW YOU'RE RUNNING UP
THE LAST FEW STEPS TO LIGHT THE
OLYMPIC FLAME.  LET THE OLYMPICS
BEGIN!  HIT THE ENTER KEY TO LIGHT
THE FLAME?


                (
               )   (
               )     (
              )  (      (
             )  )  )   (
            )  (      )  (
            )   )       (   (
            )  (    )  (       (
           MMMMMMMMMMMMMMMMM
           MMMMMMMMMMMMMMMMMM
          MMMMMMMMMMMMMMMMMMM
              MMMMMMMMMM
             MMMMMMMMMM
              MMMMMMMM
              MMMMMMMM
               MMMMM
               MMMMM
                MMMM
                MMMM
                 MM
                 MM
```

☐ Program Listing

```
10 REM CARRY THE TORCH
100 PRINT
110 PRINT "YOU'VE CARRIED THE OLYMPIC FLAME"
120 PRINT "DOWN THE FINAL STRETCH TO THE"
130 PRINT "STADIUM.  NOW YOU'RE RUNNING UP"
140 PRINT "THE LAST FEW STEPS TO LIGHT THE"
150 PRINT "OLYMPIC FLAME.  LET THE OLYMPICS"
```

(continued)

```
160  PRINT "BEGIN!   HIT THE ENTER KEY TO LIGHT"
170  PRINT "THE FLAME";
180  INPUT X$
190  PRINT
200  PRINT TAB(19);"("
210  PRINT TAB(18);")   ("
220  PRINT TAB(17);")    ("
230  PRINT TAB(16);") (    ("
240  PRINT TAB(15);") ) )  ("
250  PRINT TAB(14);") (   )  ("
260  PRINT TAB(14);") )    (  ("
270  PRINT TAB(13);") (   ) (    ("
280  FOR A=1 TO 3
290  PRINT TAB(11);
300  FOR B=1 TO 18
310  PRINT "M";
320  NEXT B
330  NEXT A
340  FOR C=1 TO 10
350  PRINT TAB(14+C/2);
360  FOR D=11-C TO 1 STEP -2
370  PRINT "MM";
380  NEXT D
390  NEXT C
```

☐ If You Have . . .

APPLE II

Add: 325 PRINT
       385 PRINT

Change: 160 PRINT "BEGIN!   HIT THE RETURN KEY TO LIGHT"
          350 PRINT TAB(14.5+C/2);

ATARI

Add: 95 DIM X$(1)
      201 GOSUB 401
      202 PRINT "("
      211 GOSUB 401
      212 PRINT ")   ("
      221 GOSUB 401
      222 PRINT ")   ("
      231 GOSUB 401
      232 PRINT ") (("
      241 GOSUB 401
      242 PRINT "))) ("
      251 GOSUB 401
      252 PRINT ") (   ) ("
      261 GOSUB 401

```
262 PRINT ")  )       (   ("
271 GOSUB 401
272 PRINT ")  (   )  (      ("
291 GOSUB 401
321 PRINT
351 GOSUB 401
381 PRINT
391 END
401 FOR F=1 TO R
402 PRINT " ";
403 NEXT F: RETURN
```

Change:
```
160 PRINT "BEGIN!   HIT THE RETURN KEY TO LIGHT"
200 R=18
210 R=17
220 R=16
230 R=15
240 R-14
250 R=13
260 R=13
270 R=12
290 R=10
350 R=(13+(C+1)/2)
```

COMMODORE 64

Add:
```
325 PRINT
385 PRINT
```

Change:
```
160 PRINT "BEGIN!   HIT THE RETURN KEY TO LIGHT"
350 PRINT TAB(14+INT(C/2+.6));
```

COMMODORE VIC-20

Delete: 260

Add:
```
325 PRINT
385 PRINT
```

Change:
```
160 PRINT "BEGIN!   HIT THE RETURN KEY TO LIGHT"
200 PRINT TAB(11);"("
210 PRINT TAB(10);")    ("
220 PRINT TAB(9);")      ("
230 PRINT TAB(8);")   (     ("
240 PRINT TAB(7);")   )  )   ("
250 PRINT TAB(6);")   (    )   ("
270 PRINT TAB(5);")   (   )  (     ("
290 PRINT TAB(3);
350 PRINT TAB(6+C/2);
```

(continued)

TEXAS INSTRUMENTS 99/4A

```
Change:  200  PRINT TAB(14);"("
         210  PRINT TAB(13);")    ("
         220  PRINT TAB(12);")     ("
         230  PRINT TAB(11);")   (    ("
         240  PRINT TAB(10);")   ) )   ("
         250  PRINT TAB(9);")  (    )   ("
         260  PRINT TAB(9);")   )    (   ("
         270  PRINT TAB(8);")  (   ) (     ("
         290  PRINT TAB(6);
         350  PRINT TAB(9+C/2);
```

TRS-80 COLOR COMPUTER

```
Add:  325  PRINT
      385  PRINT
```

```
Change:  200  PRINT TAB(14);"("
         210  PRINT TAB(13);")    ("
         220  PRINT TAB(12);")     ("
         230  PRINT TAB(11);")   (    ("
         240  PRINT TAB(10);")   ) )   ("
         250  PRINT TAB(9);")  (    )   ("
         260  PRINT TAB(9);")   )    (   ("
         270  PRINT TAB(8);")  (   ) (     ("
         290  PRINT TAB(6);
         340  FOR I=1 TO 5
         350  PRINT TAB(12+C/2);
         360  FOR D=6-C TO 1 STEP -2
```

Olympic Years

The Olympic Games are held every four years. But can you tell whether
a particular year in the future — say, the year you'll turn 18 — will have
Olympic Games? This program can. And since Olympic years are also
United States presidential election years and leap years, you'll be able to find
out about those, too.
Did you know that the sixth Olympic Games were never held, because of
World War I — and that Games XII and XIII were canceled during World War II?

☐ Sample Run

```
WILL A YEAR IN THE FUTURE
BE AN OLYMPIC YEAR?

TO FIND OUT, JUST ENTER THE
YEAR YOU WANT TO CHECK? 1987

SORRY: NO OLYMPICS IN 1987

RUN

WILL A YEAR IN THE FUTURE
BE AN OLYMPIC YEAR?

TO FIND OUT, JUST ENTER THE
YEAR YOU WANT TO CHECK? 2004

THE YEAR 2004
WILL HAVE OLYMPICS NUMBER 28.
```

☐ Program Listing

```
10 REM OLYMPIC YEARS
100 PRINT
110 PRINT "WILL A YEAR IN THE FUTURE"
120 PRINT "BE AN OLYMPIC YEAR?"
130 PRINT
140 PRINT "TO FIND OUT, JUST ENTER THE"
150 PRINT "YEAR YOU WANT TO CHECK";
160 INPUT YEAR
170 PRINT
180 IF YEAR>1983 THEN 210
190 PRINT "I SAID A YEAR IN THE FUTURE!"
200 GOTO 160
210 IF INT(YEAR/4)=YEAR/4 THEN 240
```

(continued)

15

```
220 PRINT "SORRY: NO OLYMPICS IN ";YEAR
230 END
240 OD=23+(YEAR-1984)/4
250 PRINT "THE YEAR ";YEAR
260 PRINT "WILL HAVE OLYMPICS NUMBER ";OD; "."
```

☐ If You Have . . .

APPLE II   No Changes Required

ATARI   No Changes Required

COMMODORE 64   No Changes Required

COMMODORE VIC-20

Change: 150 PRINT "YEAR YOU WANT TO CHECK"

TEXAS INSTRUMENTS 99/4A   No Changes Required

TRS-80 COLOR COMPUTER   No Changes Required

Olympic Rings

The Games are about to begin, and this program will put the Olympic symbol right in the middle of your screen. You'll have to supply the Olympic theme music yourself!

Sample Run

```
THE OLYMPICS ARE ABOUT TO START!

HIT THE ENTER KEY TO SEE THE RINGS
ON YOUR SCOREBOARD?
```

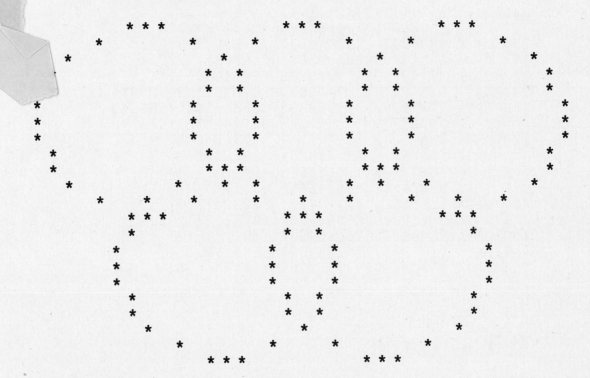

☐ Program Listing

```
10 REM OLYMPIC RINGS
100 PRINT
110 PRINT "THE OLYMPICS ARE ABOUT TO START!"
120 PRINT
130 PRINT "HIT THE ENTER KEY TO SEE THE RINGS"
140 PRINT "ON YOUR SCOREBOARD";
150 INPUT X$
```

(continued)

```
160 PRINT CHR$(12)
170 DIM T(16)
180 FOR Y=1 TO 16
190 READ T(Y)
200 NEXT Y
210 FOR A=1 TO 16
220 READ A$
230 FOR Z=1 TO T(A)
240 FOR B=1 TO LEN(A$)
250 IF VAL(MID$(A$,B,1))>5 THEN 280
260 PRINT "*";
270 GOTO 290
280 PRINT CHR$(32);
290 NEXT B
300 PRINT
310 NEXT Z
320 NEXT A
330 END
340 DATA 1,1,1,2,3,1,1,1,1,1,1,3,2,1,1,1
350 DATA 8888888843266666665427777777315
360 DATA 99999938888846665777771999399993
370 DATA 66662888888881666666666637777777774
380 DATA 77739999999970828888888465666666660
390 DATA 88577777777749993999992881999999992
400 DATA 77739999999970828888888465666666660
410 DATA 77727777777713288888842177777777775
420 DATA 88880888888177274777756266388888883
430 DATA 6666661772773666577388288817722774
440 DATA 8888888843266666665427777777315
450 DATA 88888888266666666661637777777774
460 DATA 66666663777777777388827777777775
470 DATA 88888888266666666661637777777771
480 DATA 88888888266666666617777777773
490 DATA 7777777777726666618880999991
500 DATA 99999999999932166666666213
```

☐ **If You Have . . .**

APPLE II

Change: 130 PRINT "HIT THE RETURN KEY TO SEE THE RINGS"
　　　　160 HOME

ATARI

　Add: 95 DIM X$(1),A$(40)
　　　　191 T(Y)=R

Change: 130 PRINT "HIT THE RETURN KEY TO SEE THE RINGS"
　　　　160 PRINT CHR$(125)

```
190  READ R
250  IF VAL(A$(B,B))>5 THEN 280
```

COMMODORE 64

```
Change:  130  PRINT "HIT THE RETURN KEY TO SEE THE RINGS"
         160  PRINT CHR$(147)
```

COMMODORE VIC-20

```
Change:  130  PRINT "HIT THE RETURN KEY TO SEE THE RINGS"
         160  PRINT CHR$(147)
         340  DATA 1,1,1,1,1,1,1,1,1,1,1,1,1,1,1,1
         350  DATA 88883388833888338888
         360  DATA 88838838388383883888
         370  DATA 88388883888838888388
         380  DATA 83888838388383888838
         390  DATA 83888838388383888838
         400  DATA 83888838388383888838
         410  DATA 88388883888838888388
         420  DATA 88838833388333883888
         430  DATA 88883388333883338888
         440  DATA 88883888838888388888
         450  DATA 88838888383888838888
         460  DATA 88838888383888838888
         470  DATA 88838888383888838888
         480  DATA 88883888838888388888
         490  DATA 88888388383883888888
         500  DATA 88888833888338888888
```

TEXAS INSTRUMENTS 99/4A

```
Change:  160  CALL CLEAR
         250  IF VAL(SEG$(A$,B,1))>5 THEN 280
         350  DATA 888884326666666654277777777315
         360  DATA 999388888466657777771999939999
         370  DATA 628888888881666666666637777777
         380  DATA 399999999708288888884656666666
         390  DATA 777777774999399999288819999
         400  DATA 399999999708288888884656666666
         410  DATA 277777777713288888842177777
         420  DATA 808888881772477777562663888
         430  DATA 666177277366657738828881772727
         440  DATA 888884326666666654277777777315
         450  DATA 888882666666666163777777774
         460  DATA 666637777777738882777777777
         470  DATA 888882666666666163777777771
         480  DATA 888888266666666617777777773
         490  DATA 777777772666661888099991
         500  DATA 999999999932166666666213
```

(continued)

TRS-80 COLOR COMPUTER

Delete: `400,420,450`

Change:
```
160 CLS
180 FOR Y=1 TO 13
210 FOR A=1 TO 13
330 GOTO 330
340 DATA 1,1,1,1,2,1,1,1,2,1,1,1,1
350 DATA 8888843266666666654277777777315
360 DATA 9993888884666577777719993999993
370 DATA 6288888888881666666666663777777777
380 DATA 3999999997082888888846566666666
390 DATA 7777777774999399999288819999999
410 DATA 2777777777132888888842177777777
430 DATA 66617727736665773882888817727774
440 DATA 8888843266666666654277777777315
460 DATA 66663777777777388827777777775
470 DATA 88888266666666661637777777771
480 DATA 888888266666666617777777773
490 DATA 777777726666618880999991
500 DATA 999999999932166666666213
```

Olympic Press Secretary

There's lots of work to be done behind the scenes at the Olympics. As the press secretary, it's your job to invite the international heads of state. If you can find them, you'll get a promotion; if you can't, you may soon be out of work!

☐ Sample Run

```
YOU'RE THE OLYMPIC PRESS SECRETARY.
YOU'RE IN CHARGE OF INVITING
WORLD LEADERS TO LOS ANGELES.

DO YOU KNOW WHERE TO FIND THEM?

HOW MANY INVITATIONS STILL
NEED TO BE SENT (3-20)? 4
MATCH THE CAPITAL WITH THE COUNTRY
TO BE AN OLYMPIC HERO.

    1 BELGRADE
    2 BERN
    3 BONN
    4 BUCHAREST
    5 BUDAPEST
    6 DRESDEN
    7 HAVANA
    8 HELSINKI
    9 LONDON
   10 MOSCOW
   11 PARIS
   12 PRAGUE
   13 ROME
   14 SEOUL
   15 SOFIA
   16 STOCKHOLM
   17 TOKYO
   18 WARSAW
   19 WASHINGTON D.C.
   20 WELLINGTON

WHICH CITY IS THE CAPITAL OF NEW ZEALAND?
ENTER THE NUMBER? 20
EXCELLENT!
--BUT STILL 3 MORE TO SEND!
```

(continued)

[There's more — when you get to the end of the program, you'll see something like this:]

```
WHICH CITY IS THE CAPITAL OF CZECHOSLOVAKIA?
ENTER THE NUMBER? 12
EXCELLENT!

YOU'RE AN OLYMPIC HERO!
YOU ARE PROMOTED TO VICE-PRESIDENT
OF THE OLYMPICS!
```

☐ Program Listing

```
10 REM OLYMPIC PRESS SECRETARY
100 DIM X(20)
110 PRINT
120 PRINT "YOU'RE THE OLYMPIC PRESS SECRETARY."
130 PRINT "YOU'RE IN CHARGE OF INVITING"
140 PRINT "WORLD LEADERS TO LOS ANGELES."
150 PRINT
160 PRINT "DO YOU KNOW WHERE TO FIND THEM?"
170 PRINT
180 PRINT "HOW MANY INVITATIONS STILL "
190 PRINT "NEED TO BE SENT (3-20)";
200 INPUT J
210 IF J<3 OR J>20 THEN 180
220 RANDOMIZE J
230 PRINT "MATCH THE CAPITAL WITH THE COUNTRY"
240 PRINT "TO BE AN OLYMPIC HERO."
250 FOR I=1 TO 40
260 READ C$
270 IF I<21 THEN 300
280 IF I<30 THEN PRINT " ";
290 PRINT I-20;C$
300 NEXT I
310 RESTORE
320 IF F<>0 THEN 370
330 R=1+INT(RND(1)*20)
340 FOR B=1 TO W
350 IF R=X(B) THEN 330
360 NEXT B
370 FOR I=1 TO R
380 READ K$
390 NEXT I
400 RESTORE
410 PRINT "WHICH CITY ";
420 PRINT "IS THE CAPITAL OF ";K$;"?"
430 PRINT "ENTER THE NUMBER";
440 INPUT L
450 IF L<1 OR L>20 THEN 250
```

```
460 IF L=R THEN 560
470 PRINT "WRONG!"
480 IF F=1 THEN PRINT "ONE MORE CHANCE:"
490 IF F=2 THEN PRINT "YOU'RE TOO LATE!"
500 IF F=2 THEN PRINT "YOU'RE FIRED!"
510 IF F=2 THEN END
520 F=F+1
530 PRINT "PRESS THE ENTER KEY TO TRY AGAIN";
540 INPUT X$
550 GOTO 250
560 PRINT "EXCELLENT!"
570 F=0
580 W=W+1
590 X(W)=R
600 IF W=J THEN 630
610 PRINT "--BUT STILL ";J-W;" MORE TO SEND!"
620 GOTO 250
630 PRINT
640 PRINT "YOU'RE AN OLYMPIC HERO!"
650 PRINT "YOU ARE PROMOTED TO VICE-PRESIDENT"
660 PRINT "OF THE OLYMPICS!"
670 DATA YUGOSLAVIA,SWITZERLAND,WEST GERMANY
680 DATA ROMANIA,HUNGARY,EAST GERMANY,CUBA,FINLAND
690 DATA ENGLAND,U.S.S.R,FRANCE,CZECHOSLOVAKIA,ITALY
700 DATA SOUTH KOREA,BULGARIA,SWEDEN
710 DATA JAPAN,POLAND,UNITED STATES,NEW ZEALAND
720 DATA BELGRADE,BERN,BONN,BUCHAREST,BUDAPEST
730 DATA DRESDEN,HAVANA,HELSINKI,LONDON,MOSCOW
740 DATA PARIS,PRAGUE,ROME,SEOUL,SOFIA
750 DATA STOCKHOLM,TOKYO
760 DATA WARSAW,WASHINGTON D.C.,WELLINGTON
```

☐ If You Have . . .

APPLE II

Delete: 220

Change:
```
290 PRINT I-20;" ";C$
530 PRINT "PRESS THE RETURN KEY TO TRY AGAIN";
```

ATARI

Delete: 220

Add:
```
95 DIM C$(15),K$(15)
```

Change:
```
290 PRINT I-20;" ";C$
330 R=1+INT(RND(0)*20)
530 PRINT "PRESS THE RETURN KEY TO TRY AGAIN";
```

(continued)

COMMODORE 64

Delete: 220

Change: 330 R=1+INT(RND(0)*20)
        530 PRINT "PRESS THE RETURN KEY TO TRY AGAIN";

COMMODORE VIC-20

Delete: 220

Add: 245 PRINT
     246 PRINT " PRESS RETURN KEY TO BEGIN"
     247 INPUT X$
     615 PRINT
     616 PRINT " PRESS RETURN TO CONTINUE"
     617 INPUT X$

Change: 190 PRINT "NEED TO BE SENT (3-20)"
        330 R=1+INT(RND(0)*20)
        430 PRINT "ENTER THE NUMBER"
        530 PRINT "PRESS RETURN TO TRY AGAIN"

TEXAS INSTRUMENTS 99/4A

Add: 285 PRINT " ";
     485 PRINT "ONE MORE CHANCE:"
     495 PRINT "YOU'RE TOO LATE!"

Change: 210 IF (J<3)+(J>20) THEN 180
        280 IF I>=30 THEN 290
        330 R=1+INT(RND*20)
        450 IF (L<1)+(L>20) THEN 250
        480 IF F<>1 THEN 490
        490 IF F<>2 THEN 520
        500 PRINT "YOU'RE FIRED!"
        510 END

TRS-80 COLOR COMPUTER

Delete: 220

Add: 245 PRINT "HIT ENTER KEY TO BEGIN ";
     246 INPUT X$
     295 IF I/2=INT(I/2) THEN PRINT ELSE PRINT TAB(13);

Change: 290 PRINT I-20;C$;
        330 R=RND(20)
        710 DATA JAPAN,POLAND,NEW ZEALAND,UNITED STATES
        760 DATA WARSAW,WELLINGTON,WASHINGTON D.C.

View From the Blimp

How many times have you wanted to pilot the blimp that seems to turn up at every major sports event? Well, now you can! Here's a blimp's-eye view of the Olympic marathon!

☐ Sample Run

```
YOU ARE PILOTING A BLIMP OVER THE
STREETS OF LOS ANGELES DURING THE
MARATHON.  CHEERING CROWDS LINE
THE WAY.

HIT THE ENTER KEY TO SEE THE VIEW ?
            GO  !    !  RAH
       RAH  !    !      GO
       HOORAY !    !  RAH
       HOORAY !    !
     HOORAY !      ! HOORAY
      HOORAY !     !  RAH
       HOORAY !    !  RAH
       RAH  !    !      GO
        RAH   !    !  RAH
       HOORAY !    !  RAH
            !    !  RAH
        GO  !    !
        GO  !    !  RAH
       RAH   !    !
         HOORAY !    !    GO
             !    !  RAH
       HOORAY !    !  RAH
          !    !
          !    !  RAH
        GO  !    !
     RAH   !    !     GO
     HOORAY !    !
       RAH   !    !  RAH
     RAH   !    !  RAH
        !    !  RAH
        !    !  RAH
     RAH   !    !  RAH
        !    !  RAH
        !    !
        !    !  RAH
       !    ! HOORAY
      !    !    GO
      !    !  RAH
      !    !  RAH
      !    ! HOORAY
      !    !    GO
      !    !
      !    !    GO
      !    !    GO

Break
```

☐ Program Listing

```
10 REM VIEW FROM THE BLIMP
100 PRINT
110 PRINT "YOU ARE PILOTING A BLIMP OVER THE"
120 PRINT "STREETS OF LOS ANGELES DURING THE"
130 PRINT "MARATHON.  CHEERING CROWDS LINE"
140 PRINT "THE WAY."
150 PRINT
160 PRINT "HIT THE ENTER KEY TO SEE THE VIEW";
170 INPUT X$
180 PRINT
190 R=15
200 G=1
210 IF R>10 AND INT(RND(1)*10)<8 THEN GOSUB 340
220 G=2
230 PRINT TAB(R);"!";TAB(R+5);"!";
240 IF R>24 OR INT(RND(1)*10)>7 THEN 260
250 GOSUB 340
260 PRINT
270 ON INT(RND(1)*3)+1 GOTO 280,290,300
280 R=R-1
290 GOTO 310
300 R=R+1
310 IF R>32 THEN R=31
320 IF R<1 THEN R=2
330 GOTO 200
340 J=INT(RND(1)*3)+1
350 IF G=1 THEN Z=R-7
360 IF G=2 THEN Z=R+7
370 IF J=1 THEN PRINT TAB(Z);"HOORAY ";
380 IF J=2 THEN PRINT TAB(Z);" RAH   ";
390 IF J=3 THEN PRINT TAB(Z);"   GO  ";
400 RETURN
```

☐ If You Have . . .

APPLE II

Change: 160 PRINT "HIT THE RETURN KEY TO SEE THE VIEW";

ATARI

```
Add:  95 DIM X$(1)
      205 Z=0
      225 IF Z=0 THEN Z=R:GOSUB 415
      365 GOSUB 415
```

```
      415 FOR T=1 TO Z
      425 PRINT " ";:NEXT T: RETURN
```

Change:
```
      160 PRINT "HIT THE RETURN KEY TO SEE THE VIEW";
      210 IF R>10 AND INT(RND(0)*10)<8 THEN GOSUB 340
      230 PRINT "!";"    !";
      240 IF R>24 OR INT(RND(0)*10)>7 THEN 260
      270 ON INT(RND(0)*3)+1 GOTO 280,290,300
      340 J=INT(RND(0)*3)+1
      360 IF G=2 THEN Z=1
      370 IF J=1 THEN PRINT "HOORAY ";
      380 IF J=2 THEN PRINT " RAH   ";
      390 IF J=3 THEN PRINT "  GO   ";
```

COMMODORE 64

Change:
```
      160 PRINT "HIT THE RETURN KEY TO SEE THE VIEW";
```


COMMODORE VIC-20

Change:
```
      160 PRINT "HIT THE RETURN KEY TO SEE THE VIEW"
      240 IF R>9 OR INT(RND(1)*10)>7 THEN 260
      310 IF R>15 THEN R=14
```


TEXAS INSTRUMENTS 99/4A

Add:
```
      215 GOSUB 340
      315 R=23
      325 R=2
      355 Z=R-7
      365 Z=R+7
      375 PRINT TAB(Z);"HOORAY ";
      385 PRINT TAB(Z);" RAH   ";
      395 PRINT TAB(Z);"  GO   ";
```

Change:
```
      190 R=10
      210 IF (R>10)*(INT(RND*10)<8) THEN 215 ELSE 220
      240 IF (R>15)+(INT(RND*10)>7) THEN 260
      270 ON INT(RND*3)+1 GOTO 280,290,300
      310 IF R<=24 THEN 320
      320 IF R>=1 THEN 330
      340 J=INT(RND*3)+1
      350 IF G<>1 THEN 360
      360 IF G<>2 THEN 370
      370 IF J<>1 THEN 380
      380 IF J<>2 THEN 390
      390 IF J<>3 THEN 400
```

(continued)

TRS-80 COLOR COMPUTER

```
Change:  210 IF R>10 AND RND(10)<8 THEN GOSUB 340
         240 IF R>15 OR RND(10)>7 THEN 260
         270 ON RND(3) GOTO 280,290,300
         310 IF R>23 THEN R=22
         340 J=RND(3)
```

How Long Is That Race?

The two most popular systems of measurement — English and metric —
can cause tremendous confusion. Which is longer — the 100-yard dash
or the 100 meters? Is a 10-kilometer run more difficult than a mile?
This program will put the answers at your fingertips.

☐ Sample Run

```
YOU KNOW HOW LONG A RACE IS
IN THE METRIC SYSTEM, BUT YOU
WANT TO KNOW HOW LONG IT IS
IN THE ENGLISH SYSTEM--OR VICE
VERSA.  I'LL BE GLAD TO HELP.

HOW IS THE RACE MEASURED:
METERS, KILOMETERS, YARDS, OR MILES? METERS

HOW MANY METERS IS THE RACE? 100

THE RACE IS 100 METERS LONG.
THAT'S 109.36 YARDS.

RUN

YOU KNOW HOW LONG A RACE IS
IN THE METRIC SYSTEM, BUT YOU
WANT TO KNOW HOW LONG IT IS
IN THE ENGLISH SYSTEM--OR VICE
VERSA.  I'LL BE GLAD TO HELP.

HOW IS THE RACE MEASURED:
METERS, KILOMETERS, YARDS, OR MILES? KILOMETERS

HOW MANY KILOMETERS IS THE RACE? 5

THE RACE IS 5 KILOMETERS LONG.
THAT'S 3.107 MILES.

RUN

YOU KNOW HOW LONG A RACE IS
IN THE METRIC SYSTEM, BUT YOU
WANT TO KNOW HOW LONG IT IS
IN THE ENGLISH SYSTEM--OR VICE
VERSA.  I'LL BE GLAD TO HELP.

HOW IS THE RACE MEASURED:
METERS, KILOMETERS, YARDS, OR MILES? MILES
```

(continued)

```
HOW MANY MILES IS THE RACE? 1

THE RACE IS 1 MILE LONG.
THAT'S 1.609 KILOMETERS.
```

☐ Program Listing

```
10 REM HOW LONG IS THAT RACE?
100 PRINT "YOU KNOW HOW LONG A RACE IS"
110 PRINT "IN THE METRIC SYSTEM, BUT YOU"
120 PRINT "WANT TO KNOW HOW LONG IT IS"
130 PRINT "IN THE ENGLISH SYSTEM--OR VICE"
140 PRINT "VERSA.  I'LL BE GLAD TO HELP."
150 PRINT
160 PRINT "HOW IS THE RACE MEASURED:"
170 PRINT "METERS, KILOMETERS, YARDS, OR MILES"
180 INPUT U$
190 T$=MID$(U$,1,2)
200 IF T$="YA" THEN C=.9144
210 IF T$="MI" THEN C=1.609
220 IF T$="ME" THEN C=1.0936
230 IF T$="KI" THEN C=.6214
240 IF T$<>"YA" AND T$<>"MI" AND T$<>"ME" AND T$<>"KI"
    THEN 160
250 PRINT
260 PRINT "HOW MANY ";U$;" IS THE RACE";
270 INPUT D
280 IF D=0 THEN 260
290 IF T$="YA" THEN S$="METERS"
300 IF T$="MI" THEN S$="KILOMETERS"
310 IF T$="ME" THEN S$="YARDS"
320 IF T$="KI" THEN S$="MILES"
330 PRINT
340 PRINT "THE RACE IS ";D;U$;" LONG."
350 PRINT "THAT'S ";D*C;" ";S$;"."
```

☐ If You Have . . .

APPLE II   No Changes Required

ATARI

Add: `95 DIM U$(10),T$(2),S$(10)`

Change: `190 T$=U$(1,2)`

COMMODORE 64   No Changes Required

COMMODORE VIC-20

Change: 260 PRINT "HOW MANY ";U$;" IS THE RACE"

TEXAS INSTRUMENTS 99/4A

```
Add:  205 CN=.9144
      215 CN=1.609
      225 CN=1.0936
      235 CN=.6214
      295 S$="METERS"
      305 S$="KILOMETERS"
      315 S$="YARDS"
      325 S$="MILES"
```

```
Change: 190 T$+SEG$(U$,1,2)
        200 IF T$<>"YA" THEN 210
        210 IF T$<>"MI" THEN 220
        220 IF T$<>"ME" THEN 230
        230 IF T$<>"KI" THEN 240
        240 IF (T$<>"YA")*(T$<>"MI")*(T$<>"ME")*(T$<>"KI")
            THEN 160
        290 IF T$<>"YA" THEN 300
        300 IF T$<>"MI" THEN 310
        310 IF T$<>"ME" THEN 320
        320 IF T$<>"KI" THEN 330
        350 PRINT "THAT'S";D*CN;S$;"."
```

TRS-80 COLOR COMPUTER   No Changes Required

Olympic Boxer

Muhammad Ali and Sugar Ray Leonard are just two of the great boxers who rose to fame at the Olympic Games. You might just join them — but you'll have to weigh in first.

☐ Sample Run

```
WHAT KIND OF BOXER ARE YOU?
WEIGH IN HERE!

HOW MANY POUNDS DO YOU WEIGH? 105

YOU WEIGH 47.61905 KILOGRAMS.

YOU WEIGH MORE THAN 0 POUNDS
(0 KILOGRAMS)
BUT NOT MORE THAN 105 POUNDS
(48 KILOGRAMS).
YOU ARE A LIGHT FLYWEIGHT BOXER.

RUN

WHAT KIND OF BOXER ARE YOU?
WEIGH IN HERE!

HOW MANY POUNDS DO YOU WEIGH? 169

YOU WEIGH 76.64398 KILOGRAMS.

YOU WEIGH MORE THAN 165 POUNDS
(75 KILOGRAMS)
BUT NOT MORE THAN 178 POUNDS
(81 KILOGRAMS).
YOU ARE A LIGHT HEAVYWEIGHT BOXER.
```

☐ Program Listing

```
10 REM OLYMPIC BOXER
100 PRINT
110 PRINT "WHAT KIND OF BOXER ARE YOU?"
120 PRINT "WEIGH IN HERE!"
130 PRINT
140 PRINT "HOW MANY POUNDS DO YOU WEIGH";
```

```
150  INPUT W
160  IF W=0 THEN 140
170  PRINT
180  IF W>178 THEN 280
190  READ T
200  IF T=81 THEN 240
210  IF W<=T*2.205 THEN 240
220  M=T
230  GOTO 190
240  FOR I=1 TO 10
250  READ C$
260  NEXT I
270  GOTO 320
280  PRINT "YOU WEIGH MORE THAN 178 POUNDS."
290  PRINT "(81 KILOGRAMS)"
300  PRINT "YOU ARE A HEAVYWEIGHT BOXER."
310  END
320  PRINT "YOU WEIGH ";W/2.205;" KILOGRAMS."
330  PRINT
340  PRINT "YOU WEIGH MORE THAN ";INT(M*2.205);" POUNDS"
350  PRINT "(";M;" KILOGRAMS)"
360  PRINT "BUT NOT MORE THAN ";INT(T*2.205);" POUNDS"
370  PRINT "(";T;" KILOGRAMS)."
380  PRINT "YOU ARE A ";C$;"WEIGHT BOXER."
390  PRINT
400  DATA 48,51,54,57,60
410  DATA 63.5,67,71,75,81
420  DATA LIGHT FLY,FLY
430  DATA BANTAM,FEATHER
440  DATA LIGHT,LIGHT WELTER,WELTER
450  DATA LIGHT MIDDLE,MIDDLE
460  DATA LIGHT HEAVY
```

☐ If You Have . . .

APPLE II   No Changes Required

ATARI

Add: `95 DIM C$(12)`

COMMODORE 64   No Changes Required

(continued)

COMMODORE VIC-20

Change: `140 PRINT "HOW MANY POUNDS DO YOU WEIGH"`

TEXAS INSTRUMENTS 99/4A   No Changes Required

TRS-80 COLOR COMPUTER   No Changes Required

What Day Is the Event?

It would be a shame to miss your one big Olympic chance just because you didn't know what day of the week your event was being held. With this program, you can help Olympic athletes from foreign countries — in five different languages.

☐ Sample Run

```
FOREIGN ATHLETES WANT TO FIND OUT WHAT
DAY THEIR EVENTS ARE BEING HELD.  AS
A GOOD OLYMPIC HOST, YOU KNOW THE
ANSWERS--BUT YOU DON'T KNOW ANY FOREIGN
LANGUAGES.  HELP IS ON THE WAY!

    1   ENGLISH
    2   SWEDISH
    3   FRENCH
    4   ITALIAN
    5   SPANISH
    6   GERMAN

SELECT A LANGUAGE BY NUMBER? 2

LANGUAGE SELECTED: SWEDISH

    1   SUNDAY
    2   MONDAY
    3   TUESDAY
    4   WEDNESDAY
    5   THURSDAY
    6   FRIDAY
    7   SATURDAY

(TO SWITCH LANGUAGES, ENTER "S"
--TO QUIT, ENTER "Q")
TO TRANSLATE A DAY OF THE WEEK,
ENTER THE CORRECT NUMBER? 5

IN SWEDISH, THURSDAY IS TORSDAG.
```

(continued)

[There's more—when you get to the end of the program, you'll see something like this:]

```
IN GERMAN, WEDNESDAY IS MITTWOCH.

    1   SUNDAY
    2   MONDAY
    3   TUESDAY
    4   WEDNESDAY
    5   THURSDAY
    6   FRIDAY
    7   SATURDAY


(TO SWITCH LANGUAGES, ENTER "S"
--TO QUIT, ENTER "Q")
TO TRANSLATE A DAY OF THE WEEK,
ENTER THE CORRECT NUMBER? Q
```

☐ Program Listing

```
10 REM WHAT DAY IS THE EVENT?
100 PRINT
110 PRINT "FOREIGN ATHLETES WANT TO FIND OUT WHAT"
120 PRINT "DAY THEIR EVENTS ARE BEING HELD.  AS"
130 PRINT "A GOOD OLYMPIC HOST, YOU KNOW THE"
140 PRINT "ANSWERS--BUT YOU DON'T KNOW ANY FOREIGN"
150 PRINT "LANGUAGES.  HELP IS ON THE WAY!"
160 PRINT
170 FOR C=1 TO 6
180 Y=C
190 GOSUB 630
200 PRINT TAB(2);C;TAB(5);F$
210 NEXT C
220 PRINT
230 PRINT "SELECT A LANGUAGE BY NUMBER";
240 INPUT L$
250 L=VAL(L$)
260 IF L<1 OR L>6 THEN 230
270 Y=L
280 GOSUB 630
290 PRINT
300 PRINT "LANGUAGE SELECTED: ";F$
310 PRINT
320 FOR X=1 TO 7
330 Y=6
340 Z=(X*6)-5
```

```
350 GOSUB 630
360 PRINT TAB(2);X;TAB(5);D$
370 NEXT X
380 PRINT
390 PRINT "(TO SWITCH LANGUAGES, ENTER ";CHR$(34);"S";
    CHR$(34)
400 PRINT "--TO QUIT, ENTER ";CHR$(34);"Q";CHR$(34);")"
410 PRINT "TO TRANSLATE A DAY OF THE WEEK,"
420 PRINT "ENTER THE CORRECT NUMBER";
430 INPUT C$
440 IF C$="Q" THEN END
450 C=VAL(C$)
460 IF C$="S" THEN 160
470 IF C>0 AND C<8 THEN 490
480 GOTO 420
490 PRINT
500 PRINT
510 Y=L
520 GOSUB 630
530 PRINT "IN ";F$;", ";
540 Y=6
550 Z=(C*6)-5
560 GOSUB 630
570 PRINT D$;" IS ";
580 Z=(C*6)-(6-L)
590 GOSUB 630
600 PRINT D$;"."
610 GOTO 310
620 REM --- READING SUBROUTINE ---
630 FOR P=1 TO Y
640 READ F$
650 NEXT P
660 FOR Q=1 TO Z
670 READ D$
680 NEXT Q
690 RESTORE
700 RETURN
710 DATA ENGLISH,SWEDISH,FRENCH,ITALIAN,SPANISH,GERMAN
720 DATA SUNDAY,SONDAG,DIMANCHE,DOMENICA,DOMINGO,SONNTAG
730 DATA MONDAY,MANDAG,LUNDI,LUNEDI,LUNES,MONTAG
740 DATA TUESDAY,TISDAG,MARDI,MARTEDI,MARTES,DIENSTAG
750 DATA WEDNESDAY,ONSDAG,MERCREDI,MERCOLEDI,MIERCOLES,
    MITTWOCH
760 DATA THURSDAY,TORSDAG,JEUDI,GIOVEDI,JUEVES;DONNERSTAG
770 DATA FRIDAY,FREDAG,VENDREDI,VENERDI,VIERNES,FREITAG
780 DATA SATURDAY,LORDAG,SAMEDI,SABATO,SABADO,SONNABEND
```

☐ If You Have . . .

APPLE II   No Changes Required

ATARI

Add: `95 DIM F$(11),D$(11),L$(1),C$(2)`

Change: `200 PRINT " ";C;"   ";F$`
`        360 PRINT " ";X;"   ";D$`
`        450 IF C$="S" THEN 160`
`        460 IF ASC(C$)<49 OR ASC(C$)>55 THEN 420`
`        470 C=VAL(C$):GOTO 490`

COMMODORE 64   No Changes Required

COMMODORE VIC-20

Change: `230 PRINT "SELECT A LANGUAGE BY NUMBER"`
`        420 PRINT "ENTER THE CORRECT NUMBER"`

TEXAS INSTRUMENTS 99/4A

Add: `445 END`
`        475 GOTO 490`

Change: `260 IF (L<1)+(L>6) THEN 230`
`        440 IF C$="Q" THEN 445 ELSE 450`
`        450 IF C$="S" THEN 160`
`        460 IF (ASC(C$)<49)+(ASC(C$)>55) THEN 420`
`        470 C=VAL(C$)`

TRS-80 COLOR COMPUTER

Delete: `220`

Olympic Coach

Training for the Olympics is hard work. Here's your own personal coach to help!

☐ Sample Run

```
NEED A COACH TO HELP YOU STICK TO
YOUR TRAINING?   I'LL BE GLAD TO HELP.

JUST HIT THE ENTER KEY?

PRACTICE!   PRACTICE!

PRACTICE!   PRACTICE!

PRACTICE!   PRACTICE!

PRACTICE!   PRACTICE!

PRACTICE!   PRACTICE!

PRACTICE!   PRACTICE!

PRACTICE!   PRACTICE!

Break
```

☐ Program Listing

```
10 REM OLYMPIC COACH
100 PRINT
110 PRINT "NEED A COACH TO HELP YOU STICK TO"
120 PRINT "YOUR TRAINING?   I'LL BE GLAD TO HELP."
130 PRINT
140 PRINT "JUST HIT THE ENTER KEY";
150 INPUT X$
160 PRINT
170 FOR I=1 TO 245
180 FOR J=1 TO 300
190 NEXT J
200 PRINT "PRACTICE!   PRACTICE!"
210 PRINT
220 NEXT I
```

☐ If You Have . . .

APPLE II

Change: `140 PRINT "JUST HIT THE RETURN KEY";`

ATARI

Add: `95 DIM X$(1)`

Change: `140 PRINT "JUST HIT THE RETURN KEY";`

COMMODORE 64

Change: `140 PRINT "JUST HIT THE RETURN KEY";`

COMMODORE VIC-20

Change: `140 PRINT "JUST HIT THE RETURN KEY"`

TEXAS INSTRUMENTS 99/4A   No Changes Required

TRS-80 COLOR COMPUTER   No Changes Required

Bronze Medal Diver

The diver is on the high board! Take a look at this bronze-medal style!

☐ Sample Run

```
THE DIVER IS ON THE BOARD!
HIT THE ENTER KEY TO SEE A
BRONZE MEDAL DIVE?

------
        !
         !
          !
           !
            !
             !
              !
               !
                !
                 !
                  !
                   !
                    !
WWWWWWWWWWWWWWWWWWWWWWWWWWWWWWWWWWWWWWWWWWWW
                 !
                 !
```

☐ Program Listing

```
10 REM BRONZE MEDAL DIVER
100 PRINT
110 PRINT "THE DIVER IS ON THE BOARD!"
120 PRINT "HIT THE ENTER KEY TO SEE A"
130 PRINT "BRONZE MEDAL DIVE";
140 INPUT X$
150 PRINT CHR$(12)
160 FOR I=1 TO 6
170 PRINT "-";
180 NEXT I
190 PRINT
```

(continued)

```
200 FOR I=7 TO 22
210 FOR J=1 TO I
220 PRINT " ";
230 NEXT J
240 PRINT "!"
250 NEXT I
260 FOR L=1 TO 38
270 PRINT "W";
280 NEXT L
290 PRINT
300 FOR I=23 TO 24
310 FOR J=1 TO I
320 PRINT " ";
330 NEXT J
340 PRINT "!"
350 NEXT I
360 PRINT
```

☐ If You Have . . .

APPLE II

```
Change:  120 PRINT "HIT THE RETURN KEY TO SEE A"
         150 HOME
```

ATARI

```
   Add:  95 DIM X$(1)
```

```
Change:  120 PRINT "HIT THE RETURN KEY TO SEE A"
         150 PRINT CHR$(125)
         260 FOR L=1 TO 36
```

COMMODORE 64

```
Change:  120 PRINT "HIT THE RETURN KEY TO SEE A"
         150 PRINT CHR$(147)
```

COMMODORE VIC-20

```
Change:  120 PRINT "HIT THE RETURN KEY TO SEE A"
         130 PRINT "BRONZE MEDAL DIVE"
         150 PRINT CHR$(147)
         200 FOR I=7 TO 18
         260 FOR L=1 TO 22
         300 FOR I=19 TO 20
```

TEXAS INSTRUMENTS 99/4A

Change: 150 CALL CLEAR
         260 FOR L=1 TO 28

TRS-80 COLOR COMPUTER

Change: 150 CLS
         200 FOR I=7 TO 15
         260 FOR L=1 TO 31
         300 FOR I=16 TO 17

Olympic Souvenirs

It's fun to meet people from other countries. But it's not always easy to figure out how much their money is worth. You can get the current rate of exchange from your local bank or the business section of a newspaper. Then this program can help you find out exactly how much that Swiss sweatshirt will cost in dollars!

☐ Sample Run

```
YOU'RE AN AMERICAN ATHLETE
AND YOU WANT TO BUY SOUVENIRS
FROM OTHER COUNTRIES' ATHLETES.

THEY TELL YOU THE PRICE
IN THEIR COUNTRY'S MONEY.
AND YOU NEED TO KNOW
HOW MANY DOLLARS TO GIVE THEM.

WHAT IS ONE UNIT OF
THE FOREIGN CURRENCY CALLED? FRANC

HOW MANY FRANCS WILL IT TAKE
TO BUY WHAT YOU WANT? 223

HOW MANY FRANCS
ARE THERE TO THE DOLLAR? 7.7

YOU NEED $28.96
TO BUY SOMETHING COSTING
223 FRANCS.

RUN

YOU'RE AN AMERICAN ATHLETE
AND YOU WANT TO BUY SOUVENIRS
FROM OTHER COUNTRIES' ATHLETES.

THEY TELL YOU THE PRICE
IN THEIR COUNTRY'S MONEY.
AND YOU NEED TO KNOW
HOW MANY DOLLARS TO GIVE THEM.

WHAT IS ONE UNIT OF
THE FOREIGN CURRENCY CALLED? DRACHMA

HOW MANY DRACHMAS WILL IT TAKE
TO BUY WHAT YOU WANT? 1000
```

```
HOW MANY DRACHMAS
ARE THERE TO THE DOLLAR? 93.4

YOU NEED $10.71
TO BUY SOMETHING COSTING
1000 DRACHMAS.
```

☐ **Program Listing**

```
10   REM OLYMPIC SOUVENIRS
100  PRINT
110  PRINT "YOU'RE AN AMERICAN ATHLETE"
120  PRINT "AND YOU WANT TO BUY SOUVENIRS"
130  PRINT "FROM OTHER COUNTRIES' ATHLETES."
140  PRINT
150  PRINT "THEY TELL YOU THE PRICE"
160  PRINT "IN THEIR COUNTRY'S MONEY."
170  PRINT "AND YOU NEED TO KNOW"
180  PRINT "HOW MANY DOLLARS TO GIVE THEM."
190  PRINT
200  PRINT "WHAT IS ONE UNIT OF"
210  PRINT "THE FOREIGN CURRENCY CALLED";
220  INPUT F$
230  IF F$="" THEN 200
240  PRINT
250  PRINT "HOW MANY ";F$;"S WILL IT TAKE"
260  PRINT "TO BUY WHAT YOU WANT";
270  INPUT C
280  IF C=0 THEN 250
290  PRINT
300  PRINT "HOW MANY ";F$;"S"
310  PRINT "ARE THERE TO THE DOLLAR";
320  INPUT D
330  IF D=0 THEN 300
340  PRINT
350  PRINT "YOU NEED $";INT(C/D*100+.5)/100
360  PRINT "TO BUY SOMETHING COSTING"
370  PRINT C;" ";F$;"S."
```

☐ **If You Have . . .**

APPLE II   No Changes Required

ATARI

Add: `95 DIM F$(20)`

COMMODORE 64   No Changes Required

COMMODORE VIC-20

```
Change: 210 PRINT "THE FOREIGN CURRENCY CALLED"
        260 PRINT "TO BUY WHAT YOU WANT"
        310 PRINT "ARE THERE TO THE DOLLAR"
```

TEXAS INSTRUMENTS 99/4A   No Changes Required

TRS-80 COLOR COMPUTER   No Changes Required

Decathlon

There are ten events in the decathlon, and they're always run in the same order. If you expect to train and win, you'd better know which ones come first and which come last!

☐ Sample Run

```
THE DECATHLON CONSISTS OF TEN EVENTS.

YOU MUST ENTER ALL THE EVENTS
IN THE RIGHT ORDER.  THE OLYMPIC
COMMITTEE WON'T WAIT FOR YOU!

A: 100 METER RUN
B: 400 METER RUN
C: 1500 METER RUN
D: 110 METER HURDLES
E: LONG JUMP
F: HIGH JUMP
G: POLE VAULT
H: JAVELIN
I: DISCUS
J: SHOTPUT

WHICH EVENT WILL YOU ENTER? A
RIGHT!   THAT'S EVENT NUMBER 1

A: 100 METER RUN
B: 400 METER RUN
C: 1500 METER RUN
D: 110 METER HURDLES
E: LONG JUMP
F: HIGH JUMP
G: POLE VAULT
H: JAVELIN
I: DISCUS
J: SHOTPUT

NOW WHICH EVENT WILL YOU ENTER? B
TOO EARLY!  IT HASN'T STARTED YET!
TRY AGAIN!
```

(continued)

[There's more—when you get to the end of the program, you'll see something like this:]

```
NOW WHICH EVENT WILL YOU ENTER? C
RIGHT!   THAT'S EVENT NUMBER 10

YOU WERE EARLY OR LATE
13 TIMES.   TRY AGAIN
IN FOUR YEARS.
```

☐ Program Listing

```
10  REM DECATHLON
100 PRINT "THE DECATHLON CONSISTS OF TEN EVENTS."
110 PRINT
120 PRINT "YOU MUST ENTER ALL THE EVENTS"
130 PRINT "IN THE RIGHT ORDER.  THE OLYMPIC"
140 PRINT "COMMITTEE WON'T WAIT FOR YOU!"
150 PRINT
160 GOSUB 500
170 FOR I=1 TO 10
180 INPUT T$
190 IF T$="" THEN 180
200 IF ASC(T$)<65 OR ASC(T$)>74 THEN 180
210 N=ASC(T$)-64
220 FOR J=1 TO N
230 READ P
240 NEXT J
250 RESTORE
260 IF P=I THEN 340
270 IF I<P THEN PRINT "TOO EARLY!  IT HASN'T STARTED YET!"
280 IF I>P THEN PRINT "YOU ALREADY FINISHED THAT ONE!"
290 PRINT "TRY AGAIN!"
300 PRINT
310 C=C+1
320 GOSUB 500
330 GOTO 180
340 PRINT "RIGHT!   THAT'S EVENT NUMBER ";I
350 PRINT
360 IF I=5 THEN PRINT "IT'S NOW THE SECOND DAY"
370 IF I=5 THEN PRINT "OF THE DECATHLON:"
380 PRINT
390 IF I<10 THEN GOSUB 500
400 NEXT I
410 IF C>1 THEN 460
420 PRINT "CONGRATULATIONS, CHAMPION!"
```

```
430 PRINT "YOU ENTERED ALL THE EVENTS"
440 PRINT "RIGHT ON TIME!"
450 END
460 PRINT "YOU WERE EARLY OR LATE"
470 PRINT C;" TIMES.  TRY AGAIN"
480 PRINT "IN FOUR YEARS."
490 END
500 FOR K=1 TO 20
510 READ E$
520 IF K>10 THEN PRINT CHR$(54+K);": ";E$
530 NEXT K
540 RESTORE
550 PRINT
560 IF I>1 THEN PRINT "NOW ";
570 PRINT "WHICH EVENT WILL YOU ENTER";
580 RETURN
590 DATA 1,5,10,6,2,4,8,9,7,3
600 DATA 100 METER RUN,400 METER RUN,1500 METER RUN
610 DATA 110 METER HURDLES,LONG JUMP,HIGH JUMP
620 DATA POLE VAULT,JAVELIN,DISCUS,SHOTPUT
```

☐ If You Have . . .

APPLE II   No Changes Required

ATARI

Add: `95 DIM T$(2),E$(20)`

COMMODORE 64   No Changes Required

COMMODORE VIC-20

Delete: `110, 150`

Change: `570 PRINT "WHICH EVENT WILL YOU ENTER"`

TEXAS INSTRUMENTS 99/4A

Add: `275 PRINT "TOO EARLY!  IT HASN'T STARTED YET!"`
`285 PRINT "YOU ALREADY FINISHED THAT ONE!"`
`365 PRINT "IT'S NOW THE SECOND DAY"`
`395 GOSUB 500`
`525 PRINT CHR$(54+K);": ";E$`
`565 PRINT "NOW ";`

(continued)

```
Change: 270  IF I>=P THEN 280
        280  IF I<=P THEN 290
        360  IF I<>5 THEN 380
        370  PRINT "OF THE DECATHLON:"
        390  IF I>=10 THEN 400
        520  IF K<=10 THEN 530
        560  IF I<=1 THEN 570
```

TRS-80 COLOR COMPUTER

```
Add:  155  PRINT "HIT ENTER KEY TO BEGIN";
      156  INPUT X$

Change: 270  IF I<P THEN PRINT "TOO EARLY!  IT HASN'T STARTED
             YET! ";
        280  IF I>P THEN PRINT "YOU ALREADY FINISHED THAT
             ONE! ";
        360  IF I=5 THEN PRINT "IT'S NOW THE SECOND DAY ";
        370  IF I=5 THEN PRINT "OF THE DECATHLON: ";
```

Equipment Manager

Somebody has to keep track of the Olympic athletic equipment, and that somebody is you! Just be careful not to forget anything — your team's future is riding on it!

☐ Sample Run

```
YOU'RE THE EQUIPMENT MANAGER
FOR THE OLYMPIC VILLAGE.

HOW MANY WEEKS HAVE YOU BEEN
DOING THIS JOB? 10

YOU MUST KEEP TRACK OF ALL
THE ATHLETIC EQUIPMENT.

THE TEAM FROM JAPAN HAS 20 MEMBERS.
EACH MEMBER HAS 4 SHIRTS.

HOW MANY SHIRTS DOES THE
TEAM FROM JAPAN HAVE? 80

GOOD GOING!
BUT YOU'RE NOT DONE YET!

THE TEAM FROM CUBA HAS 26 MEMBERS.
EACH MEMBER HAS 2 PAIRS OF SOCKS.

HOW MANY SOCKS DOES THE
TEAM FROM CUBA HAVE? 52

YOU ONLY COUNTED HALF THE FEET!
TRY AGAIN!
HOW MANY SOCKS DOES THE
TEAM FROM CUBA HAVE? 104

GOOD GOING!
BUT YOU'RE NOT DONE YET!

THE TEAM FROM EAST GERMANY HAS 119 MEMBERS.
EACH MEMBER HAS 8 SHIRTS.

HOW MANY SHIRTS DOES THE
TEAM FROM EAST GERMANY HAVE? 952

GOOD GOING!
THE TEAMS AWARD YOU A GOLD MEDAL
FOR YOUR WORK!
```

☐ Program Listing

```
10 REM EQUIPMENT MANAGER
100 PRINT
110 PRINT "YOU'RE THE EQUIPMENT MANAGER"
120 PRINT "FOR THE OLYMPIC VILLAGE."
130 PRINT
140 PRINT "HOW MANY WEEKS HAVE YOU BEEN"
150 PRINT "DOING THIS JOB";
160 INPUT R
170 RANDOMIZE R
180 PRINT
190 PRINT "YOU MUST KEEP TRACK OF ALL"
200 PRINT "THE ATHLETIC EQUIPMENT."
210 M=20+INT(RND(1)*100)
220 PRINT
230 FOR Z=1 TO INT(1+(RND(1)*20))
240 READ C$
250 NEXT Z
260 RESTORE
270 FOR I=1 TO 21+INT(RND(1)*4)
280 READ D$
290 NEXT I
300 RESTORE
310 PRINT "THE TEAM FROM ";C$;" HAS ";M;" MEMBERS."
320 S=2+INT(RND(1)*4)
330 PRINT "EACH MEMBER HAS ";
340 IF I<24 THEN PRINT S*2;" ";D$;"."
350 IF I>23 THEN PRINT S;" PAIRS OF ";D$;"."
360 PRINT
370 PRINT "HOW MANY ";D$;" DOES THE"
380 PRINT "TEAM FROM ";C$;" HAVE";
390 INPUT PS
400 IF PS=0 THEN 370
410 PRINT
420 IF PS=S*M*2 THEN 580
430 IF F=2 THEN 490
440 IF Z>2 AND PS=S*M THEN PRINT "YOU ONLY COUNTED HALF
    THE FEET!"
450 IF PS<>S*M THEN PRINT "NO!"
460 PRINT "TRY AGAIN!"
470 F=F+1
480 GOTO 370
490 PRINT
500 PRINT "THE RIGHT ANSWER WAS ";S*M*2;"!"
510 PRINT "YOU LOST TRACK OF THE ";D$;","
520 PRINT "SO THE TEAM FROM ";C$
530 PRINT "LOST ON THE TRACK!"
540 PRINT
550 PRINT "YOU'RE FIRED!"
560 PRINT
570 END
580 W=W+1
```

```
590 PRINT "GOOD GOING!"
600 IF W=3 THEN 640
610 F=0
620 PRINT "BUT YOU'RE NOT DONE YET!"
630 GOTO 210
640 PRINT "THE TEAMS AWARD YOU A GOLD MEDAL"
650 PRINT "FOR YOUR WORK!"
660 PRINT
670 DATA U.S.A.,U.S.S.R.,EAST GERMANY,WEST GERMANY
680 DATA JAPAN,POLAND,BULGARIA,CUBA,FINLAND,SWEDEN
690 DATA BRITAIN,ITALY,CZECHOSLOVAKIA,FRANCE
700 DATA YUGOSLAVIA,NEW ZEALAND,SOUTH KOREA
710 DATA SWITZERLAND,DENMARK,ROMANIA
720 DATA SHIRTS,JACKETS,SHOES,SOCKS
```

☐ If You Have . . .

APPLE II

Delete: 170

ATARI

Delete: 170

Add: `95 DIM C$(16),D$(11)`

Change:
```
210 M=20+INT(RND(Ø)*100)
230 FOR Z=1 TO INT(1+(RND(Ø)*20))
270 FOR I=1 TO 21+INT(RND(Ø)*4)
320 S=2+INT(RND(Ø)*4)
```

COMMODORE 64

Delete: 170

Change:
```
210 M=20+INT(RND(Ø)*100)
230 FOR Z=1 TO INT(1+(RND(Ø)*20))
270 FOR I=1 TO 21+INT(RND(Ø)*4)
320 S=2+INT(RND(Ø)*4)
```

COMMODORE VIC-20

Delete: 170

Change:
```
150 PRINT "DOING THIS JOB"
210 M=20+INT(RND(Ø)*100)
```

(continued)

```
230 FOR Z=1 TO INT(1+(RND(Ø)*2Ø))
270 FOR I=1 TO 21+INT(RND(Ø)*4)
320 S=2+INT(RND(Ø)*4)
380 PRINT "TEAM FROM ";C$;" HAVE"
```

TEXAS INSTRUMENTS 99/4A

```
Add:    345 PRINT S*2;" ";D$;"."
        355 PRINT S;" PAIRS OF ";D$;"."
        445 PRINT "YOU ONLY COUNTED HALF THE FEET!"
        455 PRINT "NO!

Change: 210 M=2Ø+INT(RND*1ØØ)
        230 FOR Z=1 TO INT(RND*2Ø)
        270 FOR I=1 TO 21+INT(RND*4)
        320 S=2+INT(RND*4)
        340 IF I>=24 THEN 350
        350 IF I<=23 THEN 360
        440 IF (Z>2)*(PS=S*M) THEN 445 ELSE 450
        450 IF PS=S*M THEN 460
```

TRS-80 COLOR COMPUTER

```
Delete: 17Ø

Change: 210 M=2Ø+RND(1ØØ)
        230 FOR Z=1 TO RND(2Ø)
        270 FOR I=1 TO 2Ø+RND(4)
        320 S=2+RND(4)
```

High Hurdles

It's you against the current world champion in the high hurdles! You're just a few steps and jumps from a gold medal . . . but can you bring it home?

☐ Sample Run

```
THIS WILL TEST HOW GOOD
A HURDLER YOU <Y> ARE.

YOUR OPPONENT IS <O>.

TO RUN FORWARD, YOU HIT
THE ENTER KEY.

BUT TO JUMP A HURDLE <HHHHHH>
YOU HAVE TO HIT THE J KEY FIRST.

AFTER EACH TURN, THE SCREEN
WILL SHOW WHETHER YOU OR YOUR
OPPONENT HIT A HURDLE OR JUMPED
TOO EARLY.  EITHER ERROR WILL
SLOW YOU DOWN.

HOW MANY TIMES HAVE YOU RUN
THE HURDLES? 24

        <HHHHHH><HHHHHH>        ? J
        <   Y  ><   O   >        ?
        <HHHHHH><HHHHHH>         ? J
        <   Y  ><   O   >        ?
        <   Y  ><   O   >        ?
        <   Y  ><   O   >EARLY   ?
        <   Y  ><   O   >        ?
        <   Y  ><   O   >        ?
        <   Y  ><   O   >        ?
        <   Y  ><   O   >        ?
        <HHHHHH><HHHHHH>         ?
  HIT   <HHHHHH><HHHHHH>         ? J
        <   Y  ><   O   >        ?
        <   Y  ><   O   >        ?
        <   Y  ><   O   >        ?
        <   Y  ><   O   >        ?
        <   Y  ><   O   >        ?
        <   Y  ><   O   >        ?

YOUR OPPONENT BEAT YOU.
BETTER LUCK NEXT TIME.
```

□ Program Listing

```
10 REM HIGH HURDLES
100 PRINT "THIS WILL TEST HOW GOOD"
110 PRINT "A HURDLER YOU <Y> ARE.",
120 PRINT
130 PRINT "YOUR OPPONENT IS <O>."
140 PRINT
150 PRINT "TO RUN FORWARD, YOU HIT"
160 PRINT "THE ENTER KEY."
170 PRINT
180 PRINT "BUT TO JUMP A HURDLE <HHHHHH>"
190 PRINT "YOU HAVE TO HIT THE J KEY FIRST."
200 PRINT
210 PRINT "AFTER EACH TURN, THE SCREEN"
220 PRINT "WILL SHOW WHETHER YOU OR YOUR"
230 PRINT "OPPONENT HIT A HURDLE OR JUMPED"
240 PRINT "TOO EARLY.  EITHER ERROR WILL"
250 PRINT "SLOW YOU DOWN."
260 PRINT
270 PRINT "HOW MANY TIMES HAVE YOU RUN"
280 PRINT "THE HURDLES";
290 INPUT R
300 RANDOMIZE R
310 M$="         "
320 PRINT CHR$(12)
330 FOR I=1 TO 20
340 IF INT(RND(1)*10)<3 THEN 380
350 PRINT TAB(7)"<   Y   >< O   >";M$;
360 H$=""
370 GOTO 400
380 H$="J"
390 PRINT TAB(7)"<HHHHHHH><HHHHHHH>";M$;
400 INPUT J$
410 IF J$<>H$ THEN 440
420 M$="         "
430 GOTO 510
440 IF H$="" THEN 480
450 PRINT "HIT";
460 H=H+1
470 GOTO 510
480 PRINT "EARLY";
490 E=E+1
500 H$=""
510 IF I=20 THEN 570
520 IF INT(RND(1)*10)>1 THEN 570
530 IF H$="" THEN FE=FE+1
540 IF H$="" THEN M$="EARLY "
550 IF H$="J" THEN FH=FH+1
560 IF H$="J" THEN M$=" HIT  "
570 NEXT I
580 PRINT
590 Y=20-H-(E/2)
```

```
600 F=20-FH-(FE/2)
610 IF Y>F THEN 660
620 IF Y=F THEN 690
630 PRINT "YOUR OPPONENT BEAT YOU."
640 PRINT "BETTER LUCK NEXT TIME."
650 END
660 PRINT "YOU WIN!"
670 PRINT "YOU'RE THE GOLD MEDAL HURDLER!"
680 END
690 PRINT "DEAD HEAT!"
700 PRINT "YOU BOTH GET GOLD MEDALS."
```

☐ If You Have . . .

APPLE II

Delete: `300`

Change:
```
160 PRINT "THE RETURN KEY."
320 HOME
```

ATARI

Delete: `300`

Add:
```
95 DIM M$(7),H$(1),J$(1)
325 R1=7
425 R1=7
455 R1=4
485 R1=2
705 END
715 FOR L=1 TO R1
725 PRINT " ";:NEXT L: RETURN
```

Change:
```
160 PRINT "THE RETURN KEY."
320 PRINT CHR$(125)
340 IF INT(RND(0)*10)<3 THEN 380
350 GOSUB 715:PRINT "<    Y   >< O    >";M$;
390 GOSUB 715:PRINT "<HHHHHHH><HHHHHHH>";M$;
520 IF INT(RND(0)*10)>1 THEN 570
```

COMMODORE 64

Delete: `300`

Change:
```
160 PRINT "THE RETURN KEY."
320 PRINT "CHR$(147)
```

(continued)

COMMODORE VIC-20

Delete: 120,140,170,200,300

Add: 315 J$="N"
     571 J$="N"
     572 NEXT I

Change: 150 PRINT "TO RUN FORWARD, YOU"
        160 PRINT "HIT THE RETURN KEY."
        180 PRINT "BUT TO JUMP A HURDLE <HHH>"
        270 PRINT "HOW MANY TIMES HAVE"
        280 PRINT "YOU RUN THE HURDLES"
        320 PRINT CHR$(147)
        340 IF INT(RND(0)*10)<3 THEN 380
        350 PRINT TAB(6) "< Y >< O >";M$
        360 H$="N"
        390 PRINT TAB(6) "<HHH><HHH>";M$
        440 IF H$="N" THEN 480
        500 H$="N"
        520 IF INT(RND(0)*10)>1 THEN 570
        530 IF H$="N" THEN FE=FE+1
        540 IF H$="N" THEN M$="EARLY "
        570 H$="N"

TEXAS INSTRUMENTS 99/4A

Add: 535 FE=FE+1
     555 FH=FH+1

Change: 320 CALL CLEAR
        340 IF INT(RND*10)<3 THEN 380
        350 PRINT TAB(6);"< Y >< O >";M$;
        390 PRINT TAB(6);"<HHHHH><HHHHH>";M$;
        520 IF INT(RND*10)>1 THEN 570
        530 IF H$<>"" THEN 550
        540 M$="EARLY "
        550 IF H$<>"J" THEN 570
        560 M$=" HIT "

TRS-80 COLOR COMPUTER

Delete: 120, 140, 170, 200, 300

Change: 320 CLS
        340 IF RND(10)<3 THEN 380
        520 IF RND(10)>1 THEN 570

Olympic Weight Lifter

Are you a flyweight, a super-heavyweight, or somewhere in between?
This program will tell you!

☐ Sample Run

```
YOU'RE A WEIGHTLIFTER--BUT WHAT
KIND DEPENDS ON HOW MUCH YOU
WEIGH.  JUST LIFT YOUR OWN
WEIGHT ONTO THESE SCALES.

HOW MANY POUNDS DO YOU WEIGH? 125

YOU WEIGH 56.68934 KILOGRAMS.

YOU WEIGH MORE THAN 123 POUNDS
(56 KILOGRAMS)
BUT NOT MORE THAN 132 POUNDS
(60 KILOGRAMS).
YOU ARE A FEATHERWEIGHT WEIGHTLIFTER.

RUN

YOU'RE A WEIGHTLIFTER--BUT WHAT
KIND DEPENDS ON HOW MUCH YOU
WEIGH.  JUST LIFT YOUR OWN
WEIGHT ONTO THESE SCALES.

HOW MANY POUNDS DO YOU WEIGH? 175

YOU WEIGH 79.36508 KILOGRAMS.

YOU WEIGH MORE THAN 165 POUNDS
(75 KILOGRAMS)
BUT NOT MORE THAN 180 POUNDS
(82 KILOGRAMS).
YOU ARE A LIGHT HEAVYWEIGHT WEIGHTLIFTER.
```

☐ **Program Listing**

```
10 REM OLYMPIC WEIGHTLIFTER
100 PRINT
110 PRINT "YOU'RE A WEIGHTLIFTER--BUT WHAT"
120 PRINT "KIND DEPENDS ON HOW MUCH YOU"
130 PRINT "WEIGH.  JUST LIFT YOUR OWN"
140 PRINT "WEIGHT ONTO THESE SCALES."
150 PRINT
160 PRINT "HOW MANY POUNDS DO YOU WEIGH";
170 INPUT W
180 IF W=0 THEN 160
190 PRINT
200 IF W>242 THEN 300
210 READ T
220 IF T=81 THEN 260
230 IF W<=T*2.205 THEN 260
240 M=T
250 GOTO 210
260 FOR I=1 TO 9
270 READ C$
280 NEXT I
290 GOTO 340
300 PRINT "YOU WEIGH MORE THAN 242 POUNDS."
310 PRINT "(100 KILOGRAMS)"
320 PRINT "YOU ARE A SUPER-HEAVYWEIGHT WEIGHTLIFTER."
330 END
340 PRINT "YOU WEIGH ";W/2.205;" KILOGRAMS."
350 PRINT
360 PRINT "YOU WEIGH MORE THAN ";INT(M*2.205);" POUNDS"
370 PRINT "(";M;" KILOGRAMS)"
380 PRINT "BUT NOT MORE THAN ";INT(T*2.205);" POUNDS"
390 PRINT "(";T;" KILOGRAMS)."
400 PRINT "YOU ARE A ";C$;"WEIGHT WEIGHTLIFTER."
410 PRINT
420 DATA 52,56,60,67,75
430 DATA 82,90,100,110
440 DATA FLY,BANTAM,FEATHER
450 DATA LIGHT,MIDDLE,LIGHT HEAVY
460 DATA MIDDLE HEAVY,100-KILO,HEAVY
```

☐ **If You Have . . .**

APPLE II   No Changes Required

ATARI

Add: `95 DIM C$(14)`

Change: `400 PRINT "YOU'RE A ";C$;"WEIGHT WEIGHTLIFTER."`

COMMODORE 64   No Changes Required

COMMODORE VIC-20

Change: `160 PRINT "HOW MANY POUNDS DO YOU WEIGH"`

TEXAS INSTRUMENTS 99/4A   No Changes Required

TRS-80 COLOR COMPUTER   No Changes Required

Olympic Trainer

Many trainers say the best way to achieve a tough goal is to do it a little bit at a time. Now you can find out exactly how much better you must do each day to reach the goal you're striving for!

☐ Sample Run

```
HOW MUCH DO YOU NEED TO IMPROVE
EACH DAY TO REACH YOUR GOAL?
I'LL HELP YOU FIND OUT!

USE COLONS AND DECIMAL POINT
TO SEPARATE THE TIME:
(3:45:20.2--NOT
3 HOURS,45 MINUTES,20.2 SECONDS)

WHAT IS YOUR CURRENT TIME
FOR THIS RACE? 4:30.2

WHAT TIME DO YOU WANT TO ACHIEVE
FOR THIS RACE?  3:49.8

HOW MANY DAYS DO YOU HAVE TO TRAIN?  150

YOU WILL NEED TO IMPROVE BY
26.93334 HUNDREDTHS OF A SECOND EACH DAY
TO ACHIEVE YOUR GOAL.

RUN

HOW MUCH DO YOU NEED TO IMPROVE
EACH DAY TO REACH YOUR GOAL?
I'LL HELP YOU FIND OUT!

USE COLONS AND DECIMAL POINT
TO SEPARATE THE TIME:
(3:45:20.2--NOT
3 HOURS,45 MINUTES,20.2 SECONDS)

WHAT IS YOUR CURRENT TIME
FOR THIS RACE? 13.3

WHAT TIME DO YOU WANT TO ACHIEVE
FOR THIS RACE? 9.8

HOW MANY DAYS DO YOU HAVE TO TRAIN? 50
```

YOU WILL NEED TO IMPROVE BY
7 HUNDREDTHS OF A SECOND EACH DAY
TO ACHIEVE YOUR GOAL.

☐ Program Listing

```
10 REM OLYMPIC TRAINER
100 PRINT
110 PRINT "HOW MUCH DO YOU NEED TO IMPROVE"
120 PRINT "EACH DAY TO REACH YOUR GOAL?"
130 PRINT "I'LL HELP YOU FIND OUT!"
140 PRINT
150 PRINT "USE COLONS AND DECIMAL POINT"
160 PRINT "TO SEPARATE THE TIME:"
170 PRINT "(3:45:20.2--NOT"
180 PRINT "3 HOURS,45 MINUTES,20.2 SECONDS)"
190 PRINT
200 FOR J=1 TO 2
210 IF J=1 THEN PRINT "WHAT IS YOUR CURRENT TIME"
220 IF J=2 THEN PRINT "WHAT TIME DO YOU WANT TO ACHIEVE"
230 PRINT "FOR THIS RACE";
240 INPUT A$
250 IF A$="" THEN 210
260 PRINT
270 N=1:F=0:S=0:M=0:H=0
280 FOR I=LEN(A$) TO 0 STEP -1
290 IF I=0 THEN 340
300 IF MID$(A$,I,1)<>"." THEN 330
310 N=0
320 GOTO 340
330 IF MID$(A$,I,1)<>":" THEN 410
340 IF N=0 THEN F=VAL(MID$(L$,1,1))
350 IF N=1 THEN S=VAL(L$)
360 IF N=2 THEN M=VAL(L$)
370 IF N=3 THEN H=VAL(L$)
380 N=N+1
390 L$=""
400 GOTO 420
410 L$=MID$(A$,I,1)+L$
420 NEXT I
430 T(J)=(H*3600)+(M*60)+S+(F/10)
440 IF T(J)=0 THEN 210
450 NEXT J
460 IF T(1)>T(2) THEN 500
470 PRINT "DO YOU WANT TO GO SLOWER?"
480 PRINT "TRY AGAIN!"
490 GOTO 200
500 PRINT "HOW MANY DAYS DO YOU HAVE TO TRAIN";
510 INPUT D
```

(continued)

```
520 PRINT
530 PRINT "YOU WILL NEED TO IMPROVE BY"
540 PRINT (T(1)-T(2))*100/D;
550 PRINT " HUNDREDTHS OF A SECOND EACH DAY"
560 PRINT "TO ACHIEVE YOUR GOAL."
570 PRINT
```

☐ If You Have . . .

APPLE II

Change: `230 PRINT "FOR THIS RACE. (ENCLOSE TIME IN QUOTES)";`

ATARI

Add:
```
95 DIM A$(11),L$(12),T(2)
375 TX=0
415 L$(TX)=A$(I,I)
```

Change:
```
300 IF A$(I,I)<>"." THEN 330
330 IF A$(I,I)<>":" THEN 410
410 TX=TX+1
```

COMMODORE 64

Change:
```
150 PRINT "USE SEMICOLONS AND DECIMAL POINT"
170 PRINT "(3;45;20.2--NOT"
330 IF MID$(A$,I,1)<>";" THEN 410
```

COMMODORE VIC-20

Change:
```
150 PRINT "USE SEMICOLONS AND DECIMAL POINT"
170 PRINT "(3;45;20.2--NOT"
230 PRINT "FOR THIS RACE"
330 IF MID$(A$,I,1)<>";" THEN 410
500 PRINT "HOW MANY DAYS DO YOU HAVE TO TRAIN"
```

TEXAS INSTRUMENTS 99/4A

Add:
```
215 PRINT "WHAT IS YOUR CURRENT TIME"
225 PRINT "WHAT TIME DO YOU WANT TO ACHIEVE"
271 F=0
272 S=0
273 M=0
274 H=0
```

```
345 F=VAL(SEG$(L$,1,1))
355 S=VAL(L$)
365 M=VAL(L$)
375 H=VAL(L$)
```

Change:
```
210 IF J<>1 THEN 220
220 IF J<>2 THEN 230
270 N=1
330 IF SEG$(A$,I,1)<>":" THEN 410
340 IF N<>0 THEN 350
350 IF N<>1 THEN 360
360 IF N<>2 THEN 370
370 IF N<>3 THEN 380
410 L$=SEG$(A$,I,1)&L$
```

TRS-80 COLOR COMPUTER

Change:
```
240 LINE INPUT A$
```

Toss the Javelin

It's a classic event — and it's right here on your computer screen! Can you change the program to let you make more than one throw each time?

☐ Sample Run

```
IT'S TIME FOR THE JAVELIN THROW.
HIT THE ENTER KEY WHEN YOU'RE READY?

THERE GOES THE JAVELIN!
```

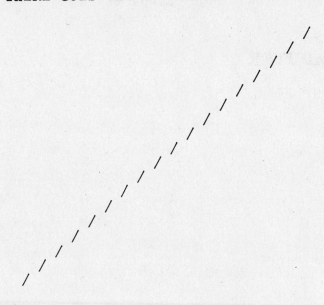

```
AND HERE IT COMES BACK DOWN!
```

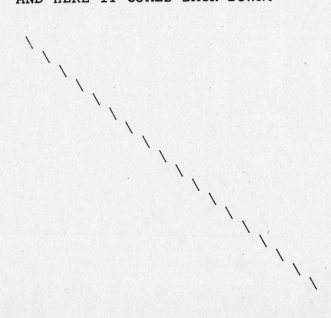

☐ Program Listing

```
10 REM TOSS THE JAVELIN
100 PRINT "IT'S TIME FOR THE JAVELIN THROW."
110 PRINT "HIT THE ENTER KEY WHEN YOU'RE READY";
120 INPUT X$
130 PRINT
140 PRINT "THERE GOES THE JAVELIN!"
150 GOSUB 320
160 GOSUB 280
170 FOR I=18 TO 1 STEP-1
180 PRINT TAB(I*2);CHR$(47)
190 NEXT I
200 GOSUB 280
210 PRINT "AND HERE IT COMES BACK DOWN!"
220 GOSUB 320
230 PRINT CHR$(12)
240 FOR I=1 TO 18
250 PRINT TAB(I*2);CHR$(92)
260 NEXT I
270 END
280 FOR I=1 TO 24
290 PRINT
300 NEXT I
310 RETURN
320 FOR D=1 TO 800
330 NEXT D
340 RETURN
```

☐ If You Have . . .

APPLE II

```
Change: 110 PRINT "HIT THE RETURN KEY WHEN YOU'RE READY";
        230 HOME
```

ATARI

```
Add: 95 DIM X$(1)
     355 FOR H=1 TO R
     365 PRINT " ";: NEXT H: RETURN
```

```
Change: 110 PRINT "HIT THE RETURN KEY WHEN YOU'RE READY";
        180 R=I*2: GOSUB 355: PRINT CHR$(47)
        230 PRINT CHR$(125)
        250 R=I*2: GOSUB 355: PRINT CHR$(92)
```

(continued)

COMMODORE 64

```
Change: 110  PRINT "HIT THE RETURN KEY WHEN YOU'RE READY";
        230  PRINT CHR$(147)
        250  PRINT TAB(I*2);CHR$(109)
```

COMMODORE VIC-20

```
Change: 110  PRINT "HIT THE RETURN KEY WHEN YOU'RE READY"
        170  FOR I=10 TO 1 STEP -1
        230  PRINT CHR$(147)
        240  FOR I=1 TO 10
        250  PRINT TAB(I*2);CHR$(109)
```

TEXAS INSTRUMENTS 99/4A

```
Change: 170  FOR I=14 TO 1 STEP-1
        230  CALL CLEAR
        240  FOR I=1 TO 14
        280  FOR I=1 TO 18
```

TRS-80 COLOR COMPUTER

```
Change: 170  FOR I=14 TO 1 STEP -1
        230  CLS
        240  FOR I=1 TO 14
```

Olympic Translator

There are lots of words that go with the Olympics. This program will let you translate an even dozen of them — into five different languages!

☐ Sample Run

```
WHAT DOES YOUR OPPONENT CALL
SOME FAMILIAR THINGS AT THE
OLYMPIC GAMES?  USE THIS PROGRAM
TO FIND OUT!

     1   ENGLISH
     2   SWEDISH
     3   FRENCH
     4   ITALIAN
     5   SPANISH
     6   GERMAN

SELECT A LANGUAGE BY NUMBER? 3

LANGUAGE SELECTED: FRENCH

     1   FIRST
     2   SECOND
     3   THIRD
     4   PRIZE
     5   GAME
     6   TEAM
     7   WIN
     8   LOSE
     9   RACE
     10  RUN
     11  JUMP
     12  PEACE

(TO SWITCH LANGUAGES, ENTER "S"
--TO QUIT, ENTER "Q")
TO TRANSLATE A WORD,
ENTER THE CORRECT NUMBER? 7

IN FRENCH, WIN IS GAGNER.
```

(continued)

[There's more — when you get to the end of the program, you'll see something like this:]

```
IN SPANISH, JUMP IS SALTAR.

      1   FIRST
      2   SECOND
      3   THIRD
      4   PRIZE
      5   GAME
      6   TEAM
      7   WIN
      8   LOSE
      9   RACE
     10   RUN
     11   JUMP
     12   PEACE

(TO SWITCH LANGUAGES, ENTER "S"
--TO QUIT, ENTER "Q")
TO TRANSLATE A WORD,
ENTER THE CORRECT NUMBER? Q
```

☐ Program Listing

```
10 REM OLYMPIC TRANSLATOR
100 PRINT
110 PRINT "WHAT DOES YOUR OPPONENT CALL"
120 PRINT "SOME FAMILIAR THINGS AT THE"
130 PRINT "OLYMPIC GAMES?   USE THIS PROGRAM"
140 PRINT "TO FIND OUT!"
150 PRINT
160 PRINT
170 FOR C=1 TO 6
180 Y=C
190 GOSUB 630
200 PRINT TAB(2);C;TAB(5);F$
210 NEXT C
220 PRINT
230 PRINT "SELECT A LANGUAGE BY NUMBER";
240 INPUT L$
250 L=VAL(L$)
260 IF L<1 OR L>6 THEN 230
270 Y=L
280 GOSUB 630
290 PRINT
300 PRINT "LANGUAGE SELECTED: ";F$
```

```
310 PRINT
320 FOR D=1 TO 12
330 Y=6
340 Z=(D*6)-5
350 GOSUB 630
360 PRINT TAB(2);D;TAB(7);WD$
370 NEXT D
380 PRINT
390 PRINT "(TO SWITCH LANGUAGES, ENTER ";CHR$(34);"S";
    CHR$(34)
400 PRINT "--TO QUIT, ENTER ";CHR$(34);"Q";CHR$(34);")"
410 PRINT "TO TRANSLATE A WORD,"
420 PRINT "ENTER THE CORRECT NUMBER";
430 INPUT C$
440 IF C$="Q" THEN END
450 C=VAL(C$)
460 IF C$="S" THEN 160
470 IF C>0 AND C<13 THEN 490
480 GOTO 380
490 PRINT
500 Y=L
510 GOSUB 630
520 PRINT "IN ";F$;", ";
530 Y=6
540 Z=(C*6)-5
550 GOSUB 630
560 PRINT WD$;" IS ";
570 Z=(C*6)-(6-L)
580 GOSUB 630
590 PRINT WD$;"."
600 PRINT
610 GOTO 310
620 REM --- READING SUBROUTINE ---
630 FOR P=1 TO Y
640 READ F$
650 NEXT P
660 FOR Q=1 TO Z
670 READ WD$
680 NEXT Q
690 RESTORE
700 RETURN
710 DATA ENGLISH,SWEDISH,FRENCH,ITALIAN,SPANISH,GERMAN
720 DATA FIRST,FORSTA,PREMIER,PRIMO,PRIMERO,ERSTE
730 DATA SECOND,ANDRA,DEUXIEME,SECONDO,SEGUNDO,ZWEITE
740 DATA THIRD,TREDJE,TROISIEME,TERZO,TERCERO,DRITTE
750 DATA PRIZE,PRIS,PRIX,PREMIO,PREMIO,PREIS
760 DATA GAME,SPEL,JEU,GIUOCO,JUEGO,SPIEL
770 DATA TEAM,LAG,EQUIPE,SQUADRA,EQUIPO,MANNSCHAFT
780 DATA WIN,VINNA,GAGNER,VINCERE,VENCER,GEWINNEN
790 DATA LOSE,FORLORA,PERDRE,PERDERE,PERDER,VERLIEREN
800 DATA RACE,TAVLING,COURSE,CORSA,CARRERA,WETTLAUF
810 DATA RUN,SPRINGA,COURIR,CORRERE,CORRER,RENNEN
820 DATA JUMP,HOPPA,SAUTER,SALTARE,SALTAR,SPRINGEN
830 DATA PEACE,FRED,PAIX,PACE,PAZ,FRIEDEN
```

☐ If You Have . . .

APPLE II   No Changes Required

ATARI

Add:
```
95 DIM C$(1),F$(11),WD$(11),L$(1)
845 FOR R1=1 TO R
855 PRINT " ";:NEXT R1:RETURN
```

Change:
```
200 R=2:GOSUB 845:PRINT C;:R=5:GOSUB 845:PRINT F$
360 R=2:GOSUB 845:PRINT D;:R=7:GOSUB 845:PRINT WD$
450 IF C$="S" THEN 160
460 IF ASC(C$)<49 OR ASC(C$)>57 THEN 420
470 C=VAL(C$):GOTO 490
```


COMMODORE 64   No Changes Required

COMMODORE VIC-20

Change:
```
230 PRINT "SELECT A LANGUAGE BY NUMBER"
420 PRINT "ENTER THE CORRECT NUMBER"
```


TEXAS INSTRUMENTS 99/4A

Add:
```
445 END
475 GOTO 490
```

Change:
```
260 IF (L<1)+(L>6) THEN 230
440 IF C$<>"Q" THEN 450
450 IF C$="S" THEN 160
460 IF (ASC(C$)<49)+(ASC(C$)>57) THEN 420
470 C=VAL(C$)
```


TRS-80 COLOR COMPUTER

Delete: 380

Olympic Travel Bureau

It's a long way to Los Angeles from foreign countries! How far exactly?
With this program, you'll have the answers in a flash!

☐ Sample Run

```
=========================================
OLYMPIC TRAVEL SERVICE MILEAGE FINDER
=========================================

YOU'RE A FOREIGN ATHLETE.
HOW FAR WILL YOU BE FLYING
TO THE LOS ANGELES 1984 GAMES?

HIT THE ENTER KEY TO BEGIN?

        1   BERLIN
        2   BUENOS AIRES
        3   CAIRO
        4   CALCUTTA
        5   CARACAS
        6   HONG KONG
        7   ISTANBUL
        8   LISBON
        9   LONDON
       10   MANILA
       11   MEXICO CITY
       12   MONTREAL
       13   MOSCOW
       14   PARIS
       15   RIO DE JANEIRO
       16   ROME
       17   SHANGHAI
       18   STOCKHOLM
       19   SYDNEY
       20   TOYKO

WHERE ARE YOU FLYING FROM? 20

FROM TOYKO TO LOS ANGELES
IS 5433 MILES BY AIR.

WANT TO TRY ANOTHER? YES

WHERE ARE YOU FLYING FROM? 3
```

(continued)

73

```
FROM CAIRO TO LOS ANGELES
IS 7520 MILES BY AIR.

WANT TO TRY ANOTHER? NO

ENJOY YOUR FLIGHT!
```

☐ Program Listing

```
10 REM OLYMPIC TRAVEL BUREAU
100 DIM D(20)
110 GOSUB 620
120 PRINT "OLYMPIC TRAVEL SERVICE MILEAGE FINDER"
130 GOSUB 620
140 PRINT
150 PRINT "YOU'RE A FOREIGN ATHLETE."
160 PRINT "HOW FAR WILL YOU BE FLYING"
170 PRINT "TO THE LOS ANGELES 1984 GAMES?"
180 PRINT
190 PRINT "HIT THE ENTER KEY TO BEGIN";
200 INPUT D$
210 PRINT
220 IF R=1 THEN RESTORE
230 PRINT
240 FOR A=1 TO 20
250 READ A$
260 PRINT TAB(5);A;TAB(9);A$
270 NEXT A
280 FOR B=1 TO 20
290 READ D(B)
300 NEXT B
310 R=1
320 PRINT
330 PRINT "WHERE ARE YOU FLYING FROM";
340 INPUT N
350 IF N<1 OR N>20 THEN 220
360 RESTORE
370 FOR C=1 TO N
380 READ A$
390 NEXT C
400 PRINT
410 PRINT "FROM ";A$;" TO LOS ANGELES"
420 PRINT "IS ";D(N);" MILES BY AIR."
430 PRINT
440 PRINT "WANT TO TRY ANOTHER";
450 INPUT Y$
460 PRINT
470 IF MID$(Y$,1,1)<>"N" THEN 220
480 PRINT "ENJOY YOUR FLIGHT!"
```

```
490 PRINT
500 END
510 DATA BERLIN,BUENOS AIRES,CAIRO,CALCUTTA
520 DATA CARACAS,HONG KONG,ISTANBUL,LISBON
530 DATA LONDON,MANILA,MEXICO CITY,MONTREAL
540 DATA MOSCOW,PARIS,RIO DE JANEIRO,ROME
550 DATA SHANGHAI,STOCKHOLM,SYDNEY,TOYKO
560 DATA 5724,6170,7520,8090
570 DATA 3632,7195,6783,5621
580 DATA 5382,7261,1589,2427
590 DATA 6003,5588,6331,6732
600 DATA 6438,5454,7530,5433
610 REM --- LINE SUBROUTINE ---
620 FOR D=1 TO 37
630 PRINT "=";
640 NEXT D
650 PRINT
660 RETURN
```

☐ If You Have . . .

APPLE II

Change:
```
190 PRINT "HIT THE RETURN KEY TO BEGIN";
```

ATARI

Add:
```
 95 DIM D$(1),A$(15),Y$(3)
261 TB=3:IF A>=10 THEN TB=2
262 GOSUB 675;PRINT A$
291 D(B)=DB
675 FOR IX=1 TO TB
685 PRINT " ";:NEXT IX:RETURN
```

Change:
```
190 PRINT "HIT THE RETURN KEY TO BEGIN";
260 TB=5:GOSUB 675:PRINT A;
290 READ DB
470 IF Y$(1,1)<>"N" THEN 220
```

COMMODORE 64

Change:
```
190 PRINT "HIT THE RETURN KEY TO BEGIN";
```

COMMODORE VIC-20

Delete: `320`

(continued)

```
Change:  190 PRINT "HIT THE RETURN KEY TO BEGIN"
         260 PRINT TAB(3);A;TAB(6);A$
         330 PRINT "WHERE ARE YOU FLYING FROM"
         620 FOR D=1 TO 21
```

TEXAS INSTRUMENTS 99/4A

```
Add:     225 RESTORE
```

```
Change:  220 IF R<>1 THEN 230
         350 IF (N<1)+(N>20) THEN 220
         470 IF SEG$(Y$,1,1)<>"N" THEN 220
         620 FOR E=1 TO 28
         640 NEXT E
```

TRS-80 COLOR COMPUTER

```
Add:  265 IF A/2=INT(A/2) THEN PRINT TAB(15);A;TAB(19);A$
```

```
Change:  260 IF A/2<>INT(A/2)THEN PRINT A;TAB(4);A$;
         540 DATA MOSCOW,PARIS,TOYKO,ROME
         550 DATA SHANGHAI,STOCKHOLM,SYDNEY,RIO DE JANEIRO
         590 DATA 6003,5588,5433,6732
         600 DATA 6438,5454,7530,6331
         620 FOR D=1 TO 31
```

Phone Home!

Making an international phone call is easy. But it's not so easy to figure out what time it is at home when you're far away. Now you can let your computer figure it out for you!

☐ Sample Run

```
YOU'RE IN LOS ANGELES.
YOU NEED TO PHONE HOME.
BUT YOU DON'T WANT TO
WAKE ANYONE UP.

WHAT TIME IS IT IN LOS ANGELES? 5:32

AM OR PM? PM

HOW MANY TIME ZONES AWAY IS HOME? 3

IS THAT EAST OR WEST OF LOS ANGELES? EAST

WHEN IT'S 5:32 PM IN LOS ANGELES,
THE TIME AT HOME IS 8:32 PM.

RUN

YOU'RE IN LOS ANGELES.
YOU NEED TO PHONE HOME.
BUT YOU DON'T WANT TO
WAKE ANYONE UP.

WHAT TIME IS IT IN LOS ANGELES? 3:22

AM OR PM? PM

HOW MANY TIME ZONES AWAY IS HOME? 5

IS THAT EAST OR WEST OF LOS ANGELES? WEST

WHEN IT'S 3:22 PM IN LOS ANGELES,
THE TIME AT HOME IS 10:22 AM.
```

□ Program Listing

```
10  REM PHONE HOME!
100 PRINT "YOU'RE IN LOS ANGELES."
110 PRINT "YOU NEED TO PHONE HOME."
120 PRINT "BUT YOU DON'T WANT TO"
130 PRINT "WAKE ANYONE UP."
140 PRINT
150 PRINT "WHAT TIME IS IT IN LOS ANGELES";
160 INPUT T$
170 IF T$="" THEN 150
180 PRINT
190 FOR I=1 TO LEN(T$)
200 IF MID$(T$,I,1)=":" THEN 250
210 IF C>0 THEN 240
220 H$=H$+MID$(T$,I,1)
230 GOTO 270
240 IF C<3 THEN M$=M$+MID$(T$,I,1)
250 C=C+1
260 B=1
270 NEXT I
280 H=VAL(H$)
290 IF H<13 AND H>0 THEN 320
300 H$=""
310 GOTO 140
320 M=VAL(M$)
330 IF M=0 THEN M$="00"
340 IF M>=0 AND M<60 THEN 370
350 M$=""
360 GOTO 140
370 PRINT "AM OR PM";
380 INPUT D$
390 IF MID$(D$,1,1)<>"A" AND MID$(D$,1,1)<>"P" THEN 370
400 PRINT
410 PRINT "HOW MANY TIME ZONES AWAY IS HOME";
420 INPUT A$
430 IF A$="" THEN 410
440 A=VAL(A$)
450 PRINT
460 IF A>12 OR A<0 THEN 410
470 PRINT "IS THAT EAST OR WEST OF LOS ANGELES";
480 INPUT E$
490 PRINT
500 Z$=MID$(E$,1,1)
510 IF Z$<>"E" AND Z$<>"W" THEN 470
520 IF Z$="E" THEN N=H+A
530 IF Z$="W" THEN N=H-A
540 PRINT "WHEN IT'S ";H$;":";M$;" ";D$;" IN LOS ANGELES,"
550 IF N<13 AND N>0 THEN 630
560 IF N<1 THEN 600
570 N=N-12
580 IF H=12 AND N<>12 THEN 700
590 GOTO 660
600 N=N+12
```

```
610 IF N=12 AND H<>12 THEN 700
620 GOTO 660
630 IF N=12 AND H<>12 THEN 660
640 IF H=12 AND Z$="W" THEN 660
650 GOTO 700
660 IF D$="PM" THEN 690
670 D$="PM"
680 GOTO 700
690 D$="AM"
700 PRINT "THE TIME AT HOME IS ";
710 PRINT N;":";
720 PRINT M$;" ";D$;"."
730 PRINT
```

☐ If You Have . . .

APPLE II

Add: `155 PRINT "(TIME MUST BE ENCLOSED IN QUOTES)"`

ATARI

Add:
```
91  DIM T$(5),H$(5),M$(3),D$(2),A$(2)
92  DIM E$(4),Z$(1)
```

Change:
```
200 IF T$(I,I)=":" THEN 250
220 H$(I)=T$(I,I)
240 IF C<3 THEN M$(C)=T$(I,I)
390 IF D$(1,1)<>"A" AND D$(1,1)<>"P" THEN 370
500 Z$=E$(1,1)
```

COMMODORE 64

Add: `155 PRINT "SEMICOLON TO SEPARATE HOURS AND MINUTES)`

Change:
```
150 PRINT "WHAT TIME IS IT IN LOS ANGELES (USE"
200 IF MID$(T$,I,1)=";" THEN 250
```

COMMODORE VIC-20

Add: `155 PRINT "SEMICOLON TO SEPARATE HOURS AND MINUTES)`

Change:
```
150 PRINT "WHAT TIME IS IT IN LOS ANGELES (USE"
200 IF MID$(T$,I,1)=";" THEN 250
370 PRINT "AM OR PM"
410 PRINT "HOW MANY TIME ZONES AWAY IS HOME"
470 PRINT "IS THAT EAST OR WEST OF LOS ANGELES"
```

(continued)

TEXAS INSTRUMENTS 99/4A

Add:
```
245 M$=M$&SEG$(T$,I,1)
335 M$="00"
525 N=H+A
535 N=H-A
```

Change:
```
200 IF SEG$(T$,I,1)=":" THEN 250
220 H$=H$&SEG$(T$,I,1)
240 IF C>=3 THEN 250
290 IF (H<13)*(H>0) THEN 320
330 IF M<>0 THEN 340
340 IF (M>=0)*(M<60) THEN 370
390 IF (SEG$(D$,1,1)<>"A")*(SEG$(D$,1,1)<>"P")
    THEN 370
460 IF (A>12)+(A<0) THEN 410
500 Z$=SEG$(E$,1,1)
510 IF (Z$<>"E")*(Z$<>"W") THEN 470
520 IF Z$<>"E" THEN 530
530 IF Z$<>"W" THEN 540
550 IF (N<13)*(N>0) THEN 630
580 IF (H=12)*(N<>12) THEN 700
610 IF (N=12)*(H<>12) THEN 700
630 IF (N=12)*(H<>12) THEN 660
640 IF (H=12)*(Z$="W") THEN 660
```

TRS-80 COLOR COMPUTER

Add:
```
160 LINE INPUT T$
```

Silver Medal Diver

How graceful! The silver medalist displays superb form!

☐ Sample Run

```
THE DIVER IS ON THE BOARD!
HIT THE ENTER KEY TO SEE
A SILVER MEDAL DIVE?
```

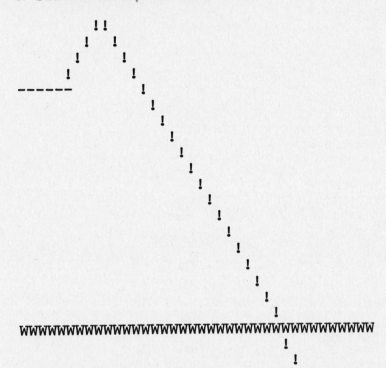

☐ Program Listing

```
10 REM SILVER MEDAL DIVER
100 PRINT
110 PRINT "THE DIVER IS ON THE BOARD"
120 PRINT "HIT THE ENTER KEY TO SEE"
130 PRINT "A SILVER MEDAL DIVE";
140 INPUT X$
150 PRINT CHR$(12)
```

(continued)

```
160 PRINT TAB(9); "!!"
170 PRINT TAB(8); "!"; TAB(11);"!"
180 PRINT TAB(7); "!"; TAB(12);"!"
190 PRINT TAB(6); "!"; TAB(13);"!"
200 FOR I=1 TO 6
210 PRINT "-";
220 NEXT I
230 PRINT TAB(14);"!"
240 FOR I=15 TO 28
250 PRINT TAB(I);"!"
260 NEXT I
270 FOR L=1 TO 38
280 PRINT "W";
290 NEXT L
300 PRINT
310 FOR I=29 TO 30
320 PRINT TAB(I);"!"
330 NEXT I
```

☐ If You Have . . .

APPLE II

Change:
```
120 "HIT THE RETURN KEY TO SEE"
150 HOME
```

ATARI

Add:
```
95 DIM X$(1)
331 END
345 FOR A=1 TO R
355 PRINT " ";:NEXT A:RETURN
```

Change:
```
120 "HIT THE RETURN KEY TO SEE"
150 PRINT CHR$(125)
160 R=9:GOSUB 345:PRINT "!!"
170 R=8:GOSUB 345:PRINT "!";:R=2:GOSUB 345:PRINT "!"
180 R=7:GOSUB 345:PRINT "!";:R=4:GOSUB 345:PRINT "!"
190 R=6:GOSUB 345:PRINT "!";:R=6:GOSUB 345:PRINT "!"
230 R=8:GOSUB 345:PRINT "!"
240 FOR I=15 TO 27
250 R=I:GOSUB 345:PRINT "!"
270 FOR L=1 TO 36
310 FOR I=28 TO 29
320 R=I:GOSUB 345:PRINT "!"
```

COMMODORE 64

```
Change:  120  PRINT "HIT THE RETURN KEY TO SEE"
         150  PRINT CHR$(147)
```

COMMODORE VIC-20

```
Change:  120  PRINT "HIT THE RETURN KEY TO SEE"
         150  PRINT CHR$(147)
         160  PRINT TAB(7); "!!"
         170  PRINT TAB(6); "!"; TAB(9);"!"
         180  PRINT TAB(5); "!"; TAB(10);"!"
         190  PRINT TAB(4); "!"; TAB(11);"!"
         200  FOR I=1 TO 4
         230  PRINT TAB(12);"!"
         240  FOR I=13 TO 19
         270  FOR L=1 TO 21
         310  FOR I=20 TO 21
```

TEXAS INSTRUMENTS 99/4A

```
Change:  150  CALL CLEAR
         240  FOR I=15 TO 26
         270  FOR L=1 TO 28
         310  FOR I=27 TO 28
```

TRS-80 COLOR COMPUTER

```
Change:  150  CLS
         240  FOR I=15 TO 20
         270  FOR L=1 TO 31
         310  FOR I=21 TO 22
```

Olympic Marathon

Outdistance the pack and you may set a new world's record. But lag behind, and you'll be lucky to pick up a bronze medal. Good luck, marathoner!

☐ Sample Run

```
THIS IS THE MARATHON!
IT'S A RACE OF 26 MILES AND 285 YARDS.

EVERY TIME YOU GET A MATH PROBLEM RIGHT
YOU MOVE AHEAD ONE MILE.

WRONG ANSWERS SLOW YOU DOWN.

AND THE GOING GETS HARDER
AS THE RACE GETS LONGER.

WHAT'S YOUR FULL NAME? ROCK RUNNER

HOW MANY TIMES HAVE YOU RUN
THE MARATHON? 20

THE MARATHON BEGINS!

AS THE RACE STARTS,
ROCK RUNNER IS IN THE LEAD.

  1  +  5 = ? 6

RIGHT!

AFTER 1 MILE
ROCK RUNNER IS IN THE LEAD.

  11  +  10 = ? 21

RIGHT!

AFTER 2 MILES
ROCK RUNNER IS IN THE LEAD.

  5  X  9 = ? 45

RIGHT!

AFTER 3 MILES
ROCK RUNNER IS IN THE LEAD.
```

```
 3  +  11 = ? 14
```

RIGHT!

AFTER 4 MILES
ROCK RUNNER IS IN THE LEAD.

```
 2  +  9 = ? 18
```

WRONG!

```
 2  +  9 =  11
```

```
 7  /  7 = ? 1
```

RIGHT!

AFTER 5 MILES
ROCK RUNNER IS 49 RUNNERS
BEHIND THE LEADER.

```
 8  -  12 = ? -4
```

RIGHT!

AFTER 6 MILES
ROCK RUNNER IS 43 RUNNERS
BEHIND THE LEADER.

```
 10  +  5 = ? 15
```

RIGHT!

[[There's more--when you get to the end of the

program, you'll see something like this:]]

```
 19  /  19 = ? 1
```

RIGHT!

AS THE RACE ENDS,
ROCK RUNNER IS IN FIRST PLACE!

CONGRATULATIONS!

THE TIME FOR ROCK RUNNER WAS:
2 HOURS, 14 MINUTES AND 11 SECONDS.

☐ Program Listing

```
10 REM OLYMPIC MARATHON
100 PRINT "THIS IS THE MARATHON!"
110 PRINT "IT'S A RACE OF 26 MILES AND 285 YARDS."
120 PRINT
130 PRINT "EVERY TIME YOU GET A MATH PROBLEM RIGHT"
140 PRINT "YOU MOVE AHEAD ONE MILE."
150 PRINT
160 PRINT "WRONG ANSWERS SLOW YOU DOWN."
170 PRINT
180 PRINT "AND THE GOING GETS HARDER"
190 PRINT "AS THE RACE GETS LONGER."
200 PRINT
210 PRINT "WHAT'S YOUR FULL NAME";
220 INPUT N$
230 IF N$="" THEN 210
240 PRINT
250 PRINT "HOW MANY TIMES HAVE YOU RUN"
260 PRINT "THE MARATHON";
270 INPUT R
280 RANDOMIZE R
290 PRINT
300 PRINT "THE MARATHON BEGINS!"
310 PRINT
320 PRINT "AS THE RACE STARTS,"
330 PRINT N$;" IS IN THE LEAD."
340 M=1
350 C=INT(RND(1)*4)+1
360 A=INT(RND(1)*13)+INT(M/3)
370 B=INT(RND(1)*13)+INT(M/3)
380 IF C<>4 THEN 410
390 IF B=0 THEN 360
400 IF A/B<>INT(A/B) THEN 360
410 IF C=1 THEN OP$=" + "
420 IF C=2 THEN OP$=" - "
430 IF C=3 THEN OP$=" X "
440 PRINT
450 IF C=4 THEN OP$=" / "
460 PRINT A;OP$;B;"= ";
470 INPUT Z$
480 IF Z$="" THEN 460
490 Z=VAL(Z$)
500 IF C=1 THEN R=A+B
510 IF C=2 THEN R=A-B
520 IF C=3 THEN R=A*B
530 IF C=4 THEN R=A/B
540 IF R<>Z THEN 580
550 PRINT "RIGHT!"
560 T=T+300-(5*M)
570 GOTO 630
580 PRINT "WRONG!"
590 PRINT A;OP$;B;"= ";R
600 PRINT
```

```
610 T=T+300+26-M
620 GOTO 350
630 PRINT
640 LT=M*300
650 IF M>26 THEN 800
660 PRINT "AFTER ";M;
670 IF M<>1 THEN 700
680 PRINT " MILE "
690 GOTO 710
700 PRINT " MILES "
710 IF T<=LT THEN 750
720 PRINT N$;" IS ";INT((T-LT)/5);" RUNNERS"
730 PRINT "BEHIND THE LEADER."
740 GOTO 760
750 PRINT N$;" IS IN THE LEAD."
760 PRINT
770 PRINT
780 M=M+1
790 GOTO 350
800 PRINT "AS THE RACE ENDS,"
810 IF LT>=T THEN 850
820 PRINT N$;" COMES IN AFTER"
830 PRINT INT((T-LT)/5);" OTHER RUNNERS."
840 GOTO 870
850 PRINT N$;" IS IN FIRST PLACE!"
860 PRINT "CONGRATULATIONS!"
870 PRINT "THE TIME FOR ";N$;" WAS:"
880 H=INT(T/3600)
890 Z=INT((T-(H*3600))/60)
900 S=T-(H*3600)-(Z*60)
910 PRINT H;" HOURS, ";Z;" MINUTES AND ";S;" SECONDS."
920 END
```

☐ If You Have . . .

APPLE II

Delete: 280

ATARI

Delete: 280

  Add: 95 DIM N$(22),Z$(5),OP$(3)

Change: 350 C=INT(RND(0)*4)+1
          360 A=INT(RND(0)*13)+INT(M/3)
          370 B=INT(RND(0)*13)+INT(M/3)   *(continued)*

COMMODORE 64

Delete: 280

Change: 350 C=INT(RND(0)*4)+1
         360 A=INT(RND(0)*13)+INT(M/3)
         370 B=INT(RND(0)*13)+INT(M/3)

COMMODORE VIC-20

Delete: 280

Change: 210 PRINT "WHAT'S YOUR FULL NAME"
         260 PRINT "THE MARATHON"
         350 C=INT(RND(0)*4)+1
         360 A=INT(RND(0)*13)+INT(M/3)
         370 B=INT(RND(0)*13)+INT(M/3)
         460 PRINT A;OP$;B;"= "

TEXAS INSTRUMENTS 99/4A

Add: 415 OP$=" + "
      425 OP$=" - "
      435 OP$=" X "
      455 OP$=" / "
      505 R=A+B
      515 R=A-B
      525 R=A*B
      535 R=A/B

Change: 350 C=INT(RND*4)+1
         360 A=INT(RND*13)+INT(M/3)
         370 B=INT(RND*13)+INT(M/3)
         410 IF C<>1 THEN 420
         420 IF C<>2 THEN 430
         430 IF C<>3 THEN 440
         450 IF C<>4 THEN 460
         500 IF C<>1 THEN 510
         510 IF C<>2 THEN 520
         520 IF C<>3 THEN 530
         530 IF C<>4 THEN 540

TRS-80 COLOR COMPUTER

Delete: 280

Change: 350 C=RND(4)
         360 A=RND(12)+INT(M/3)
         370 B=RND(12)+INT(M/3)

Medal Grapher

Which country has earned the most medals overall? Which country is mining the silver, and which is getting the gold? Now you'll be able to compare four countries' records at a glance. This program automatically puts the teams with the most medals at the top — and the ones with the fewest at the bottom. It makes a gorgeous graph of each country's medal record, too!

☐ Sample Run

```
WANT TO COMPARE DIFFERENT COUNTRIES'
RECORDS?  THIS MAKES IT EASY TO
PRINT A GRAPH OF MEDALS FOR FOUR
DIFFERENT COUNTRIES.

ENTER THE NAME OF COUNTRY NUMBER 1? HUNGARY
HOW MANY GOLD MEDALS? 4
HOW MANY SILVER MEDALS? 5
HOW MANY BRONZE MEDALS? 12

ENTER THE NAME OF COUNTRY NUMBER 2? ITALY
HOW MANY GOLD MEDALS? 2
HOW MANY SILVER MEDALS? 7
HOW MANY BRONZE MEDALS? 4

ENTER THE NAME OF COUNTRY NUMBER 3? JAPAN
HOW MANY GOLD MEDALS? 9
HOW MANY SILVER MEDALS? 6
HOW MANY BRONZE MEDALS? 10

ENTER THE NAME OF COUNTRY NUMBER 4? UNITED STATES
HOW MANY GOLD MEDALS? 34
HOW MANY SILVER MEDALS? 35
HOW MANY BRONZE MEDALS? 25

UNITED STATES --  94 TOTAL MEDALS
GGGGGGGGGGGGGGGGGGGGGGGGGGGGGGGGGG
SSSSSSSSSSSSSSSSSSSSSSSSSSSSSSSSSSS
BBBBBBBBBBBBBBBBBBBBBBBBB

JAPAN --  25 TOTAL MEDALS
GGGGGGGGG
SSSSSS
BBBBBBBBBB

HUNGARY --  21 TOTAL MEDALS
GGGG
SSSSS
BBBBBBBBBBBB
```

(continued)

```
ITALY --   13 TOTAL MEDALS
GG
SSSSSSS
BBBB
```

☐ **Program Listing**

```
10 REM MEDAL GRAPHER
100 PRINT
110 PRINT "WANT TO COMPARE DIFFERENT COUNTRIES'"
120 PRINT "RECORDS?  THIS MAKES IT EASY TO"
130 PRINT "PRINT A GRAPH OF MEDALS FOR FOUR"
140 PRINT "DIFFERENT COUNTRIES."
150 PRINT
160 FOR I=1 TO 4
170 PRINT "ENTER THE NAME OF COUNTRY NUMBER ";I;":"
180 IF I=1 THEN INPUT F$
190 IF I=1 AND F$="" THEN 170
200 IF I=2 THEN INPUT S$
210 IF I=2 AND S$="" THEN 170
220 IF I=3 THEN INPUT T$
230 IF I=3 AND T$="" THEN 170
240 IF I=4 THEN INPUT L$
250 IF I=4 AND L$="" THEN 170
260 PRINT "HOW MANY GOLD MEDALS";
270 INPUT G$
280 IF G$="" THEN 260
290 G(I)=VAL(G$)
300 PRINT "HOW MANY SILVER MEDALS";
310 INPUT SM$
320 IF SM$="" THEN 300
330 S(I)=VAL(SM$)
340 PRINT "HOW MANY BRONZE MEDALS";
350 INPUT B$
360 IF B$="" THEN 340
370 B(I)=VAL(B$)
380 PRINT
390 NEXT I
400 GOSUB 640
410 FOR I=1 TO 4
420 IF C(I)=1 THEN PRINT F$;
430 IF C(I)=2 THEN PRINT S$;
440 IF C(I)=3 THEN PRINT T$;
450 IF C(I)=4 THEN PRINT L$;
460 PRINT " -- "; P(I); " TOTAL MEDALS"
470 FOR J=1 TO G(C(I))
480 PRINT "G";
490 NEXT J
500 PRINT
510 FOR J=1 TO S(C(I))
520 PRINT "S";
```

```
530 NEXT J
540 PRINT
550 FOR J=1 TO B(C(I))
560 PRINT "B";
570 NEXT J
580 IF I<4 THEN PRINT
590 PRINT
600 C=C+1
610 NEXT I
620 PRINT
630 END
640 FOR I=1 TO 4
650 P(I)=G(I)+S(I)+B(I)
660 C(I)=I
670 NEXT I
680 FOR I=1 TO 3
690 FOR J=I+1 TO 4
700 IF P(I)>P(J) THEN 770
710 T=P(I)
720 P(I)=P(J)
730 P(J)=T
740 T=C(I)
750 C(I)=C(J)
760 C(J)=T
770 NEXT J
780 NEXT I
790 RETURN
```

☐ If You Have . . .

APPLE II

Add: `385 PRINT`

ATARI

Add: `91  DIM F$(17),S$(17),T$(17),L$(17),G$(3),SM$(3),`
      `    B$(3)`
      `92  DIM G(4),S(4),B(4),C(4),P(4)`

COMMODORE 64   No Changes Required

COMMODORE VIC-20

Change: `260 PRINT "HOW MANY GOLD MEDALS"`
         `300 PRINT "HOW MANY SILVER MEDALS"`
         `340 PRINT "HOW MANY BRONZE MEDALS"`   *(continued)*

91

TEXAS INSTRUMENTS 99/4A

```
Add:   185 INPUT F$
       205 INPUT S$
       225 INPUT T$
       245 INPUT L$
       425 PRINT F$
       435 PRINT S$
       445 PRINT T$
       455 PRINT L$
       585 PRINT

Change: 180 IF I<>1 THEN 200
        190 IF F$="" THEN 170
        200 IF I<>2 THEN 210
        210 IF S$="" THEN 170
        220 IF I<>3 THEN 240
        230 IF T$="" THEN 170
        240 IF I<>4 THEN 260
        250 IF L$="" THEN 170
        420 IF C(I)<>1 THEN 430
        430 IF C(I)<>2 THEN 440
        440 IF C(I)<>3 THEN 450
        450 IF C(I)<>4 THEN 460
        580 IF I>=4 THEN 590
        600 D=D+1
```

TRS-80 COLOR COMPUTER   No Changes Required

Pentathlons

There's not just one pentathlon in the Olympic Games — there are two! Each one has five events, but they're very different. If you know the answers here, you're a true Olympic expert!

☐ Sample Run

```
THERE ARE TWO OLYMPIC EVENTS WITH
ALMOST THE SAME NAME.

ONE IS A COMPETITION
FOR WOMEN: THE PENTATHLON.

THE OTHER IS A COMPETITION
FOR MEN: THE MODERN PENTATHLON.

EACH HAS FIVE EVENTS.
WIN OUR PENTATHLON
BY TELLING WHICH ARE WHICH.

IS LONG JUMP
A MODERN PENTATHLON EVENT
OR A PENTATHLON EVENT--
ENTER M OR P? P
RIGHT!
THAT MAKES 1 RIGHT.

IS RIDING
A MODERN PENTATHLON EVENT
OR A PENTATHLON EVENT--
ENTER M OR P? M
RIGHT!
THAT MAKES 2 RIGHT.

IS FENCING
A MODERN PENTATHLON EVENT
OR A PENTATHLON EVENT--
ENTER M OR P? M
RIGHT!
THAT MAKES 3 RIGHT.

IS 100 METER HURDLES
A MODERN PENTATHLON EVENT
OR A PENTATHLON EVENT--
ENTER M OR P? M
SORRY!
THAT'S A PENTATHLON EVENT.
THAT'S 1 WRONG.
```

(continued)

```
IS 200 METER RUN
A MODERN PENTATHLON EVENT
OR A PENTATHLON EVENT--
ENTER M OR P? P
RIGHT!
THAT MAKES 9 RIGHT.


YOU GOT 9 RIGHT
AND 1 WRONG.
YOU'LL HAVE TO SETTLE FOR A
SILVER MEDAL.
```

☐ **Program Listing**

```
10 REM PENTATHLONS
100 PRINT "THERE ARE TWO OLYMPIC EVENTS WITH"
110 PRINT "ALMOST THE SAME NAME."
120 PRINT
130 PRINT "ONE IS A COMPETITION"
140 PRINT "FOR WOMEN: THE PENTATHLON."
150 PRINT
160 PRINT "THE OTHER IS A COMPETITION"
170 PRINT "FOR MEN: THE MODERN PENTATHLON."
180 PRINT
190 PRINT "EACH HAS FIVE EVENTS."
200 PRINT "WIN OUR PENTATHLON"
210 PRINT "BY TELLING WHICH ARE WHICH."
220 FOR I=1 TO 10
230 GOSUB 580
240 PRINT
250 PRINT "IS ";E$
260 PRINT "A MODERN PENTATHLON EVENT"
270 PRINT "OR A PENTATHLON EVENT--"
280 PRINT "ENTER M OR P";
290 INPUT A$
300 IF A$<>"P" AND A$<>"M" THEN 280
310 IF A$=P$ THEN 400
320 PRINT "SORRY!"
330 PRINT "THAT'S A ";
340 IF P$="M" THEN PRINT "MODERN "
350 PRINT "PENTATHLON EVENT."
360 W=W+1
370 PRINT
380 PRINT "THAT'S ";W;" WRONG."
390 GOTO 430
```

```
400 PRINT "RIGHT!"
410 R=R+1
420 PRINT "THAT MAKES ";R;" RIGHT."
430 NEXT I
440 PRINT
450 IF R=10 THEN 550
460 PRINT "YOU GOT ";R;" RIGHT"
470 PRINT "AND ";W;" WRONG."
480 IF R<7 THEN PRINT "MAYBE YOU SHOULD WATCH"
490 IF R<7 THEN PRINT "THE OLYMPICS ON TV."
500 IF R=7 THEN PRINT "TRY AGAIN IN FOUR YEARS."
510 IF R>7 AND R<10 THEN PRINT "YOU'LL HAVE TO SETTLE FOR A"
520 IF R=8 THEN PRINT " BRONZE MEDAL."
530 IF R=9 THEN PRINT " SILVER MEDAL."
540 END
550 PRINT "A PERFECT SCORE!"
560 PRINT "YOU WIN THE GOLD MEDAL!"
570 END
580 FOR K=1 TO I
590 READ P$
600 NEXT K
610 FOR L=1 TO 10
620 READ E$
630 NEXT L
640 RESTORE
650 RETURN
660 DATA P,M,M,P,M,M,P,P,M,P
670 DATA LONG JUMP,RIDING,FENCING,100 METER HURDLES
680 DATA CROSS-COUNTRY RUN,SHOOTING,HIGH JUMP
690 DATA SHOT PUT,300 METER SWIMMING,200 METER RUN
```

☐ If You Have . . .

APPLE II   No Changes Required

ATARI

Add: `95 DIM E$(20),A$(1),P$(20)`

COMMODORE 64   No Changes Required

COMMODORE VIC-20

Delete: `120`

Change: `280 PRINT "ENTER M OR P"`

(continued)

TEXAS INSTRUMENTS 99/4A

```
Add:  345 PRINT "MODERN "
      485 PRINT "MAYBE YOU SHOULD WATCH."
      505 PRINT "TRY AGAIN IN FOUR YEARS."
      515 PRINT "YOU'LL HAVE TO SETTLE FOR A"
      525 PRINT " BRONZE MEDAL."
      535 PRINT " SILVER MEDAL."
```

```
Change:  300 IF (A$<>"P")*(A$<>"M") THEN 280
         340 IF P$<>"M" THEN 350
         480 IF R>6 THEN 500
         490 PRINT "THE OLYMPICS ON TV."
         500 IF R<>7 THEN 510
         510 IF (R<=7)+(R>=10) THEN 520
         520 IF R<>8 THEN 530
         530 IF R<>9 THEN 540
```

TRS-80 COLOR COMPUTER

```
Delete:  150
```

```
Change:  100 PRINT "THERE ARE TWO OLYMPIC EVENTS"
         110 PRINT "WITH ALMOST THE SAME NAME."
```

Track and Field Record Book — Men

Want the men's Olympic track and field records at your fingertips?
This program will give you all the current records — like lightning!
This program includes records set at the 1980 Olympics. To keep your
program up to date in 1984, just change the proper DATA statements. But be
sure your new DATA statements have exactly the same number of commas as
the old ones — otherwise, you'll set a record for wrong answers!

☐ Sample Run

```
=== OLYMPIC TRACK AND FIELD RECORDS ===

 1   100-M DASH          2   200-M DASH
 3   400-M DASH          4   800-M RUN
 5   1500-M RUN          6   5000-M RUN
 7   10000-M RUN         8   MARATHON
 9   110-M HURDLES      10   400-M HURDLES
11   3000-M STPLCHS     12   20000-M WALK
13   50000-M WALK       14   400-M RELAY
15   1600-M RELAY       16   HIGH JUMP
17   LONG JUMP          18   TRIPLE JUMP
19   POLE VAULT         20   SHOT PUT
21   DISCUS             22   JAVELIN
23   HAMMER THROW       24   DECATHLON


==========================================


TO SEE THE CURRENT OLYMPIC RECORD,
ENTER THE NUMBER OF THE EVENT? 16


========= OLYMPIC RECORD BOOK =========

EVENT: HIGH JUMP

YEAR: 1980

RECORD HOLDER: GERD WESSIG

COUNTRY: EAST GERMANY

OLYMPIC RECORD: 7 FT 8-3/4 IN


==========================================
```

(continued)

WANT TO LOOK UP ANOTHER RECORD? YES

TO SEE THE CURRENT OLYMPIC RECORD,
ENTER THE NUMBER OF THE EVENT? 1

========= OLYMPIC RECORD BOOK =========

EVENT: 100-METER DASH

YEAR: 1968

RECORD HOLDER: JAMES HINES

COUNTRY: USA

OLYMPIC RECORD: 9.9 SEC

===

WANT TO LOOK UP ANOTHER RECORD? NO

☐ Program Listing

```
10 REM TRACK AND FIELD RECORD BOOK - MEN
100 PRINT CHR$(12)
110 PRINT "=== OLYMPIC TRACK AND FIELD RECORDS ==="
120 PRINT
130 FOR C=1 TO 24 STEP 2
140 R=C
150 S=5
160 GOSUB 650
170 PRINT C;TAB(5);R1$;
180 R=C+1
190 GOSUB 650
200 PRINT TAB(20);C+1;TAB(24);R1$
210 NEXT C
220 PRINT
230 GOSUB 570
240 PRINT
250 PRINT "TO SEE THE CURRENT OLYMPIC RECORD,"
260 PRINT "ENTER THE NUMBER OF THE EVENT";
270 INPUT N$
280 N=VAL(N$)
290 IF N<1 OR N>24 THEN 250
300 PRINT CHR$(12)
```

```
310 PRINT "========= OLYMPIC RECORD BOOK ========="
320 PRINT
330 R=N
340 GOSUB 650
350 FOR'F=1 TO 6
360 IF MID$(R1$,F,2)<>"-M" THEN 380
370 R1$=MID$(R1$,1,F+1)+"ETER"+MID$(R1$,F+2,LEN(R1$)-F)
380 NEXT F
390 IF N<>11 THEN 410
400 R1$="3000-METER STEEPLECHASE"
410 PRINT "EVENT: ";R1$
420 PRINT
430 PRINT "YEAR: ";R2$
440 PRINT
450 PRINT "RECORD HOLDER: ";R3$
460 PRINT
470 PRINT "COUNTRY: ";R4$
480 PRINT
490 PRINT "OLYMPIC RECORD: ";R5$
500 PRINT
510 GOSUB 570
520 PRINT "WANT TO LOOK UP ANOTHER RECORD";
530 INPUT Y$
540 IF MID$(Y$,1,1)<>"N" THEN 100
550 END
560 REM --- LINE AND SPACE SUBROUTINE ---
570 FOR F=1 TO 39
580 PRINT "=";
590 NEXT F
600 FOR G=1 TO 3
610 PRINT
620 NEXT G
630 RETURN
640 REM --- READING SUBROUTINE ---
650 FOR Q=1 TO R
660 READ R1$,R2$,R3$,R4$,R5$
670 NEXT Q
680 RESTORE
690 RETURN
700 DATA 100-M DASH,1968,JAMES HINES,USA,9.9 SEC
710 DATA 200-M DASH,1968,TOMMIE SMITH,USA,19.8 SEC
720 DATA 400-M DASH,1968,LEE EVANS,USA,43.8 SEC
730 DATA 800-M RUN,1976,ALBERTO JUANTORENA,CUBA,1 MIN
    43.5 SEC
740 DATA 1500-M RUN,1968,KIPCHOGE KEINO,KENYA,3 MIN
    34.9 SEC
750 DATA 5000-M RUN,1980,MIRUTS YIFTER,ETHIOPIA,13 MIN
    21 SEC
760 DATA 10000-M RUN,1972,LASSE VIREN,FINLAND,27 MIN
    38.4 SEC
770 DATA MARATHON,1976,WALTER CIERPINSKI,EAST GERMANY,
    2 HRS 9 MIN 55 SEC
780 DATA 110-M HURDLES,1972,RODNEY MILBURN,USA,13.24 SEC
790 DATA 400-M HURDLES,1976,EDWIN MOSES,USA,47.6 SEC
```

(continued)

```
800 DATA 3000-M STPLCHS,1976,ANDERS GARDERUD,SWEDEN,8 MIN
    8.02 SEC
810 DATA 20000-M WALK,1980,MAURIZIO DAMILIANO,ITALY,1 HR
    23 MIN 35.5 SEC
820 DATA 50000-M WALK,1980,HARTWIG GAUDER,EAST GERMANY,
    3 HRS 49 MIN 24 SEC
830 DATA 400-M RELAY,1972,(TEAM),USA,38.19 SEC
840 DATA 1600-M RELAY,1968,(TEAM),USA,2 MIN 56.1 SEC
850 DATA HIGH JUMP,1980,GERD WESSIG,EAST GERMANY,7 FT
    8-3/4 IN
860 DATA LONG JUMP,1968,BOB BEAMON,USA,29 FT 2-1/2 IN
870 DATA TRIPLE JUMP,1968,VIKTOR SANEYEV,USSR,57 FT 3/4 IN
880 DATA POLE VAULT,1980,WLADYSLAW KOZAKIEWICZ,POLAND,18 FT
    11-1/2 IN
890 DATA SHOT PUT,1980,VLADIMIR KISELYOV,USSR,70 FT 1/2 IN
900 DATA DISCUS,1976,MAC WILKINS,USA,221 FT 5 IN
910 DATA JAVELIN,1976,MIKLOS NEMETH,HUNGARY,310 FT 4 IN
920 DATA HAMMER THROW,1980,YURI SEDYKH,USSR,268 FT 4-1/2 IN
930 DATA DECATHLON,1976,BRUCE JENNER,USA,8618 PTS
```

☐ If You Have . . .

APPLE II

Change: 100 HOME
         300 HOME

ATARI

```
Add:  91   DIM R1$(25),R2$(4),R3$(22),R4$(17),R5$(22)
      92   DIM N$(2),Y$(3),R1A$(11)
      169  IDX=3:GOSUB 945
      171  IF C>=10 THEN IDX=2
      172  GOSUB 945:PRINT R1$;
      185  IDX=(16-(LEN(R1$))):GOSUB 945
      201  IF C+1>=10 THEN IDX=2
      202  GOSUB 945:PRINT R1$
      371  IF N=11 THEN 390
      373  PRINT "EVENT: ";R1$;"ETER";R1A$
      374  GOTO 420
      401  PRINT "EVENT: ";R1$
      402  GOTO 420
      945  FOR A=1 TO IDX
      955  PRINT " ";:NEXT A:RETURN
```

```
Change:  100  PRINT CHR$(125)
         170  PRINT C;
         200  PRINT C+1;:IDX=3
```

```
300 PRINT CHR$(125)
360 IF R1$(F,F+1)<>"-M" THEN 380
370 R1A$=R1$(F+2,LEN(R1$)):R1$=R1$(1,F+1)
380 NEXT F
540 IF Y$(1,1)<>"N" THEN 100
570 FOR F=1 TO 37
900 DATA DISCUS ,1976,MAC WILKINS,USA,221 FT 5 IN
```

COMMODORE 64

Change:
```
100 PRINT CHR$(147)
300 PRINT CHR$(147)
```

COMMODORE VIC-20

Add:
```
205 IF C=13 THEN PRINT "HIT THE RETURN KEY TO SEE
    OTHER RECORDS"
206 IF C=13 THEN INPUT D$
```

Change:
```
100 PRINT CHR$(147)
170 PRINT C;TAB(5);R1$
200 PRINT C+1;TAB(5);R1$
260 PRINT "ENTER THE NUMBER OF THE EVENT"
300 PRINT CHR$(147)
310 PRINT "=OLYMPIC RECORD BOOK="
520 PRINT "WANT TO LOOK UP ANOTHER RECORD"
570 FOR F=1 TO 21
```

TEXAS INSTRUMENTS 99/4A

Delete: 600, 610, 620, 800

Add:
```
815 DATA 1 HR 23 MIN 35.5 SEC
825 DATA 3 HRS 49 MIN 24 SEC
945 DATA 3000-M STPLCHS,1976,ANDERS GARDERUD,SWEDEN
946 DATA 8 MIN 8.02 SEC
```

Change:
```
100 CALL CLEAR
200 PRINT TAB(15);C+1;TAB(19);R1$
290 IF (N<1)+(N>24) THEN 250
300 CALL CLEAR
360 IF SEG$(R1$,F,2)<>"-M" THEN 380
370 R1$=SEG$(R1$,1,F+1)&"ETER"&SEG$(R1$,F+2,
    LEN(R1$)-F)
540 IF SEG$(Y$,1,1)<>"N" THEN 100
570 FOR F=1 TO 28
760 DATA 10000-M RN,1972,LASSE VIREN,FINLAND,27
    MIN 38.4 SEC
780 DATA 110-M HRDL,1972,RODNEY MILBURN,USA,13.24
    SEC
790 DATA 400-M HRDL,1976,EDWIN MOSES,USA,47.6 SEC
```

(continued)

```
810 DATA 20000-M WK,1980,MAURIZIO DAMILIANO,ITALY
820 DATA 50000-M WK,1980,HARTWIG GAUDER,EAST GERMANY
830 DATA 400-M RLY,1972,(TEAM),USA,38.19 SEC
840 DATA 1600-M RLY,1968,(TEAM),USA,2 MIN 56.1 SEC
870 DATA TRPL JUMP,1968,VIKTOR SANEYEV,USSR,57 FT
    3/4 IN
920 DATA HMER THROW,1980,YURI SEDYKH,USSR,268 FT
    4-1/2 IN
```

TRS-80 COLOR COMPUTER

Delete: `220, 240, 600, 610, 620`

Add:
```
815 DATA 1 HR 23 MIN 35.5 SEC
825 DATA 3 HRS 49 MIN 24 SEC
```

Change:
```
100 CLS
110 PRINT "OLYMPIC TRACK AND FIELD RECORDS";
170 PRINT C;TAB(3);R1$;
200 PRINT TAB(15);C+1;TAB(17);R1$
250 PRINT "TO SEE CURRENT OLYMPIC RECORD,"
300 CLS
310 PRINT "==== OLYMPIC RECORD BOOK ===="
570 FOR F=1 TO 32
780 DATA 110-M HRDLES,1972,RODNEY MILBURN,USA,13.24
    SEC
790 DATA 400-M HRDLES,1976,EDWIN MOSES,USA,47.6 SEC
810 DATA 20000-M WLK,1980,MAURIZIO DAMILIANO,ITALY
820 DATA 50000-M WLK,1980,HARTWIG GAUDER,EAST
    GERMANY
840 DATA 1600-M RELY,1968,(TEAM),USA,2 MIN 56.1 SEC
920 DATA HAMMER THRW,1980,YURI SEDYKH,USSR,268 FT
    4-1/2 IN
```

Track and Field Record Book — Women

If you've already typed in the men's record book, you'll have this program running in no time! Just delete the DATA statements for the men and enter the statements for women. Then change lines 10, 130, 290, 390 and 400 to match those lines here. Your new record book should work just fine.

☐ Sample Run

```
=== OLYMPIC TRACK AND FIELD RECORDS ===

     1   100-M DASH        2   200-M DASH
     3   400-M DASH        4   800-M RUN
     5   1500-M RUN        6   100-M HURDLES
     7   400-M RELAY       8   1600-M RELAY
     9   HIGH JUMP        10   LONG JUMP
    11   SHOT PUT         12   DISCUS
    13   JAVELIN          14   PENTATHLON


==========================================


TO SEE THE CURRENT OLYMPIC RECORD,
ENTER THE NUMBER OF THE EVENT? 9


========= OLYMPIC RECORD BOOK =========

EVENT: HIGH JUMP

YEAR: 1980

RECORD HOLDER: SARA SIMEONI

COUNTRY: ITALY

OLYMPIC RECORD: 6 FT 5-1/2 IN

==========================================


WANT TO LOOK UP ANOTHER RECORD? Y


TO SEE THE CURRENT OLYMPIC RECORD,
ENTER THE NUMBER OF THE EVENT? 13
```

(continued)

```
========= OLYMPIC RECORD BOOK =========

EVENT: JAVELIN

YEAR: 1980

RECORD HOLDER: MARIA COLON

COUNTRY: CUBA

OLYMPIC RECORD: 224 FT 5 IN

==========================================


WANT TO LOOK UP ANOTHER RECORD? N
```

☐ Program Listing

```
10 REM TRACK AND FIELD RECORD BOOK -- WOMEN
100 PRINT CHR$(12)
110 PRINT "=== OLYMPIC TRACK AND FIELD RECORDS ==="
120 PRINT
130 FOR C=1 TO 14 STEP 2
140 R=C
150 S=5
160 GOSUB 650
170 PRINT C;TAB(5);R1$;
180 R=C+1
190 GOSUB 650
200 PRINT TAB(20);C+1;TAB(24);R1$
210 NEXT C
220 PRINT
230 GOSUB 570
240 PRINT
250 PRINT "TO SEE THE CURRENT OLYMPIC RECORD,"
260 PRINT "ENTER THE NUMBER OF THE EVENT";
270 INPUT N$
280 N=VAL(N$)
290 IF N<1 OR N>14 THEN 250
300 PRINT CHR$(12)
310 PRINT "========= OLYMPIC RECORD BOOK ========="
320 PRINT
330 R=N
340 GOSUB 650
350 FOR F=1 TO 6
360 IF MID$(R1$,F,2)<>"-M" THEN 380
370 R1$=MID$(R1$,1,F+1)+"ETER"+MID$(R1$,F+2,LEN(R1$)-F)
```

```
380 NEXT F
390 REM THIS LINE AND THE NEXT MUST BE
400 REM CHANGED FROM THE MEN'S RECORD PROGRAM
410 PRINT "EVENT: ";R1$
420 PRINT
430 PRINT "YEAR: ";R2$
440 PRINT
450 PRINT "RECORD HOLDER: ";R3$
460 PRINT
470 PRINT "COUNTRY: ";R4$
480 PRINT
490 PRINT "OLYMPIC RECORD: ";R5$
500 PRINT
510 GOSUB 570
520 PRINT "WANT TO LOOK UP ANOTHER RECORD";
530 INPUT Y$
540 IF MID$(Y$,1,1)<>"N" THEN 100
550 END
560 REM --- LINE AND SPACE SUBROUTINE ---
570 FOR F=1 TO 39
580 PRINT "=";
590 NEXT F
600 FOR G=1 TO 3
610 PRINT
620 NEXT G
630 RETURN
640 REM --- READING SUBROUTINE ---
650 FOR Q=1 TO R
660 READ R1$,R2$,R3$,R4$,R5$
670 NEXT Q
680 RESTORE
690 RETURN
700 DATA 100-M DASH,1960 (AND 1968),WILMA RUDOLPH (&
    WYOMIA TYUS),USA,11 SEC
710 DATA 200-M DASH,1980,BARBARA WOCKEL,EAST GERMANY,22.03
    SEC
720 DATA 400-M DASH,1980,MARITA KOCH,EAST GERMANY,48.88
    SEC
730 DATA 800-M RUN,1980,NADEZHDA OLIZARENKO,USSR,1 MIN
    53.5 SEC
740 DATA 1500-M RUN,1976,TATIANA KAZANKINA,USSR,4 MIN 5.48
    SEC
750 DATA 100-M HURDLES,1980,VERA KOMISOVA,USSR,12.56 SEC
760 DATA 400-M RELAY,1980,(TEAM),EAST GERMANY,41.60 SEC
770 DATA 1600-M RELAY,1976,(TEAM),EAST GERMANY,3 MIN 19.23
    SEC
780 DATA HIGH JUMP,1980,SARA SIMEONI,ITALY,6 FT 5-1/2 IN
790 DATA LONG JUMP,1980,TATIANA KOLPAKOVA,USSR,23 FT 2 IN
800 DATA SHOT PUT,1980,ILONA SLUPLANEK,USSR,73 FT 6 IN
810 DATA DISCUS,1980,EVELIN JAHL,EAST GERMANY,229 FT 6 1/2
    IN
820 DATA JAVELIN,1980,MARIA COLON,CUBA,224 FT 5 IN
830 DATA PENTATHLON,1964,IRINA PRESS,USSR,5246 PTS
```

☐ If You Have . . .

APPLE II

Change: 100 HOME
             300 HOME

ATARI

```
Add:   91 DIM R1$(25),R2$(15),R3$(30),R4$(17),R5$(22)
       92 DIM N$(2),Y$(3),R1A$(11)
       169 IDX=3: GOSUB 855
       171 IF C>=10 THEN IDX=2
       172 GOSUB 855:PRINT R1$;
       185 IDX=(16-(LEN(R1$))):GOSUB 855
       201 IF C+1>=10 THEN IDX=2
       202 GOSUB 855:PRINT R1$
       371 IF N=11 THEN 390
       373 PRINT "EVENT: ";R1$;"ETER";R1A$
       374 GOTO 420
       401 PRINT "EVENT: ";R1$
       402 GOTO 420
       855 FOR A=1 TO IDX
       865 PRINT " ";:NEXT A:RETURN
```

```
Change:  100  PRINT CHR$(125)
         170  PRINT C;
         200  PRINT C+1;:IDX=3
         300  PRINT CHR$(125)
         360  IF R1$(F,F+1)<>"-M" THEN 380
         370  R1A$=R1$(F+2,LEN(R1$)):R1$=R1$(1,F+1)
         380  NEXT F
         540  IF Y$(1,1)<>"N" THEN 100
         570  FOR F=1 TO 37
```

COMMODORE 64

```
Change:  100  PRINT CHR$(147)
         300  PRINT CHR$(147)
```

COMMODORE VIC-20

Delete: 240

```
Change:  100  PRINT CHR$(147)
         170  PRINT C;TAB(5);R1$
         200  PRINT C+1;TAB(5);R1$
         260  PRINT "ENTER THE NUMBER OF THE EVENT"
         300  PRINT CHR$(147)
         310  PRINT "= OLYMPIC RECORD BOOK ="
         520  PRINT "WANT TO LOOK UP ANOTHER RECORD"
```

106

```
570 FOR F=1 TO 21
600 FOR G=1 TO 2
```

TEXAS INSTRUMENTS 99/4A

Add:
```
195 IF (C<>7) THEN 200
196 PRINT
197 PRINT C+1;TAB(5);Rl$
198 GOTO 210
```

Change:
```
100 CALL CLEAR
200 PRINT TAB(15);C+1;TAB(19);Rl$
290 IF (N<1) + (N>14) THEN 250
300 CALL CLEAR
360 IF SEG$(Rl$,F,2)<>"-M" THEN 380
370 Rl$=SEG$(Rl$,1,F+1)&"ETER"&SEG$(Rl$,F+2,
    LEN(Rl$)-F)
540 IF SEG$(Y$,1,1)<>"N" THEN 100
570 FOR F=1 TO 28
```

TRS-80 COLOR COMPUTER

Delete: 390, 400, 600, 610, 620

Change:
```
100 CLS
110 PRINT "OLYMPIC TRACK AND FIELD RECORDS"
170 PRINT C;TAB(3);Rl$;
200 PRINT TAB(15);C+1;TAB(17);Rl$
250 PRINT "TO SEE CURRENT OLYMPIC RECORD,"
300 CLS
310 PRINT "===== OLYMPIC RECORD BOOK ====="
570 FOR F=1 TO 32
```

Swimming and Diving Record Book

Here are all the important Olympic swimming and diving records. Choose one, and you won't believe how fast it appears on your screen! Remember: You can update the DATA statements during or after the 1984 Olympics. Check a newspaper or almanac for the facts.

☐ Sample Run

```
ENTER "M" FOR MEN'S RECORDS
OR "W" FOR WOMEN'S RECORDS? M

=== MEN'S OLYMPIC SWIMMING RECORDS ===

    1   100-METER FREESTYLE
    2   200-METER FREESTYLE
    3   400-METER FREESTYLE
    4   1500-METER FREESTYLE
    5   100-METER BACKSTROKE
    6   200-METER BACKSTROKE
    7   100-METER BREASTSTROKE
    8   200-METER BREASTSTROKE
    9   100-METER BUTTERFLY
   10   200-METER BUTTERFLY
   11   400-METER INDIV MEDLEY
   12   800-METER FREESTYLE RELAY
   13   400-METER MEDLEY RELAY
   14   SPRINGBOARD DIVE
   15   PLATFORM DIVE


==========================================


TO SEE THE CURRENT OLYMPIC RECORD,
ENTER THE NUMBER NEXT TO THE EVENT? 9

====== MEN'S OLYMPIC RECORD BOOK ======

EVENT: 100-METER BUTTERFLY

YEAR: 1972

RECORD HOLDER: MARK SPITZ

COUNTRY: USA

OLYMPIC RECORD: 54.27 SEC

==========================================
```

WANT TO LOOK UP ANOTHER RECORD? YES

    ENTER "M" FOR MEN'S RECORDS
    OR "W" FOR WOMEN'S RECORDS? W

== WOMEN'S OLYMPIC SWIMMING RECORDS ==

        1   100-METER FREESTYLE
        2   200-METER FREESTYLE
        3   400-METER FREESTYLE
        4   800-METER FREESTYLE
        5   100-METER BACKSTROKE
        6   200-METER BACKSTROKE
        7   100-METER BREASTSTROKE
        8   200-METER BREASTSTROKE
        9   100-METER BUTTERFLY
       10   200-METER BUTTERFLY
       11   400-METER INDIV MEDLEY
       12   400-METER FREESTYLE RELAY
       13   400-METER MEDLEY RELAY
       14   SPRINGBOARD DIVE
       15   PLATFORM DIVE

==

TO SEE THE CURRENT OLYMPIC RECORD,
ENTER THE NUMBER NEXT TO THE EVENT? 4

===== WOMEN'S OLYMPIC RECORD BOOK =====

EVENT: 800-METER FREESTYLE

YEAR: 1980

RECORD HOLDER: MICHELLE FORD

COUNTRY: AUSTRALIA

OLYMPIC RECORD: 8 MIN 28.9 SEC

==

WANT TO LOOK UP ANOTHER RECORD? NO

☐ Program Listing

```
10 REM SWIMMING AND DIVING RECORD BOOK
100 PRINT CHR$(12)
110 MW=0
120 FOR S=1 TO 3
130 PRINT
140 NEXT S
150 PRINT TAB(5);"ENTER ";CHR$(34);"M";CHR$(34);" FOR MEN'S
    RECORDS"
160 PRINT TAB(5);"OR ";CHR$(34);"W";CHR$(34);" FOR WOMEN'S
    RECORDS";
170 INPUT R$
180 PRINT CHR$(12)
190 IF R$="M" THEN 250
200 IF R$="W" THEN 220
210 GOTO 100
220 PRINT "== WOMEN'S OLYMPIC SWIMMING RECORDS =="
230 MW=15
240 GOTO 260
250 PRINT "=== MEN'S OLYMPIC SWIMMING RECORDS ==="
260 PRINT
270 FOR E=1 TO 15
280 R=E+MW
290 GOSUB 810
300 PRINT TAB(3);E;TAB(8);R1$
310 NEXT E
320 PRINT
330 GOSUB 740
340 PRINT
350 PRINT "TO SEE THE CURRENT OLYMPIC RECORD,"
360 PRINT "ENTER THE NUMBER NEXT TO THE EVENT";
370 INPUT N$
380 N=VAL(N$)
390 IF N<1 OR N>15 THEN 180
400 PRINT CHR$(12)
410 R=N+MW
420 GOSUB 810
430 IF R$="W" THEN 560
440 PRINT "====== MEN'S OLYMPIC RECORD BOOK ======"
450 PRINT
460 PRINT "EVENT: ";R1$
470 PRINT
480 PRINT "YEAR: ";R2$
490 PRINT
500 PRINT "RECORD HOLDER: ";R3$
510 PRINT
520 PRINT "COUNTRY: ";R4$
530 PRINT
540 PRINT "OLYMPIC RECORD: ";R5$
550 GOTO 670
560 PRINT "===== WOMEN'S OLYMPIC RECORD BOOK ====="
570 PRINT
580 PRINT "EVENT: ";R1$
```

```
590 PRINT
600 PRINT "YEAR: ";R2$
610 PRINT
620 PRINT "RECORD HOLDER: ";R3$
630 PRINT
640 PRINT "COUNTRY: ";R4$
650 PRINT
660 PRINT "OLYMPIC RECORD: ";R5$
670 PRINT
680 GOSUB 740
690 PRINT "WANT TO LOOK UP ANOTHER RECORD";
700 INPUT Y$
710 IF MID$(Y$,1,1)<>"N" THEN 110
720 END
730 REM --- LINE AND SPACE SUBROUTINE ---
740 FOR F=1 TO 39
750 PRINT "=";
760 NEXT F
770 PRINT
780 PRINT
790 RETURN
800 REM --- READING SUBROUTINE ---
810 FOR Q=1 TO R
820 READ R1$,R2$,R3$,R4$,R5$
830 NEXT Q
840 RESTORE
850 RETURN
860 DATA 100-METER FREESTYLE,1976,JIM MONTGOMERY,USA,
    49.99 SEC
870 DATA 200-METER FREESTYLE,1980,SERGEI KOPLIAKOV,USSR,1
    MIN 49.81 SEC
880 DATA 400-METER FREESTYLE,1980,VLADIMIR SALNIKOV,USSR,
    3 MIN 51.31 SEC
890 DATA 1500-METER FREESTYLE,1980,VLADIMIR SALNIKOV,USSR,
    14 MIN 58.27 SEC
900 DATA 100-METER BACKSTROKE,1976,JOHN NABER,USA,55.49
    SEC
910 DATA 200-METER BACKSTROKE,1976,JOHN NABER,USA,1 MIN
    59.19 SEC
920 DATA 100-METER BREASTSTROKE,1976,JOHN HENCKEN,USA,1
    MIN 3.11 SEC
930 DATA 200-METER BREASTSTROKE,1976,DAVID WILLKIE,BRITAIN,
    2 MIN 15.11 SEC
940 DATA 100-METER BUTTERFLY,1972,MARK SPITZ,USA,54.27 SEC
950 DATA 200-METER BUTTERFLY,1976,MIKE BRUNER,USA,1 MIN
    59.23 SEC
960 DATA 400-METER INDIV MEDLEY,1980,ALEKSANDR SIDORENKO,
    USSR,4 MIN 22.8 SEC
970 DATA 800-METER FREESTYLE RELAY,1976,(TEAM),USA,7 MIN
    23.22 SEC
980 DATA 400-METER MEDLEY RELAY,1976,(TEAM),USA,3 MIN
    42.22 SEC
990 DATA SPRINGBOARD DIVE,1980,ALEXSANDR PORTNOV,USSR,
    905.02 PTS
```

(continued)

```
1000 DATA PLATFORM DIVE,1980,FALK HOFFMAN,E GERMANY,835.65
     PTS
1010 DATA 100-METER FREESTYLE,1980,BARBARA KRAUSE,E GERMANY,
     54.79 SEC
1020 DATA 200-METER FREESTYLE,1980,BARBARA KRAUSE,E GERMANY,
     1 MIN 58.33 SEC
1030 DATA 400-METER FREESTYLE,1980,INES DIERS,E GERMANY,4
     MIN 8.76 SEC
1040 DATA 800-METER FREESTYLE,1980,MICHELLE FORD,AUSTRALIA,
     8 MIN 28.9 SEC
1050 DATA 100-METER BACKSTROKE,1980,RICA REINISCH,E GERMANY,
     1 MIN 0.86 SEC
1060 DATA 200-METER BACKSTROKE,1980,RICA REINISCH,E GERMANY,
     2 MIN 11.77 SEC
1070 DATA 100-METER BREASTSTROKE,1980,UTE GEWENIGER,E
     GERMANY,1 MIN 10.22 SEC
1080 DATA 200-METER BREASTSTROKE,1980,LINA KACHUSHITE,USSR,
     2 MIN 29.54 SEC
1090 DATA 100-METER BUTTERFLY,1976,KORNELIA ENDER,E GERMANY,
     1 MIN 0.13 SEC
1100 DATA 200-METER BUTTERFLY,1980,INES GEISSLER,E GERMANY,
     2 MIN 10.44 SEC
1110 DATA 400-METER INDIV MEDLEY,1980,PETRA SCHNEIDER,E
     GERMANY,4 MIN 36.29 SEC
1120 DATA 400-METER FREESTYLE RELAY,1980,(TEAM),E GERMANY,
     3 MIN 42.71 SEC
1130 DATA 400-METER MEDLEY RELAY,1980,(TEAM),E GERMANY,4
     MIN 6.67 SEC
1140 DATA SPRINGBOARD DIVE,1980,IRINA KALININA,USSR,725.91
     PTS
1150 DATA PLATFORM DIVE,1980,MARTINA JASCHKE,E GERMANY,
     596.25 PTS
```

☐ If You Have . . .

APPLE II

```
Change:  100  HOME
         180  HOME
         400  HOME
```

ATARI

```
Add:  91   DIM R1$(27),R2$(4),R3$(22),R4$(17),R5$(22)
      92   DIM R$(1),H$(2),Y$(3)
      149  IDX=4
      155  PRINT " FOR MEN'S RECORDS";
      165  PRINT " FOR WOMEN'S RECORDS";
```

```
301 IDX=3:IF E>=10 THEN IDX=2
302 GOSUB 1165: PRINT R1$
1165 FOR A=1 TO IDX
1175 PRINT " ";:NEXT A:RETURN
```

Change:
```
100  PRINT CHR$(125)
150  GOSUB 1165: PRINT "ENTER ";CHR$(34);"M";
     CHR$(34);
160  GOSUB 1165: PRINT "OR ";CHR$(34);"W";CHR$(34);
180  PRINT CHR$(125)
300  IDX=2:GOSUB 1165:PRINT E;
400  PRINT CHR$(125)
710  IF Y$(1,1)<>"N" THEN 110
740  FOR F=1 TO 37
```

COMMODORE 64

Change:
```
100  PRINT CHR$(147)
180  PRINT CHR$(147)
400  PRINT CHR$(147)
```

COMMODORE VIC-20

Add:
```
165  PRINT " FOR WOMEN'S RECORDS"
305  IF E=8 THEN PRINT "HIT RETURN FOR OTHER
     RECORDS"
306  IF E=8 THEN INPUT D$
```

Change:
```
100  PRINT CHR$(147)
160  PRINT TAB(5);"OR ";CHR$(34);"W";CHR$(34);
180  PRINT CHR$(147)
300  PRINT E; TAB(4); R1$
360  PRINT "ENTER THE NUMBER NEXT TO THE EVENT"
400  PRINT CHR$(147)
690  PRINT "WANT TO LOOK UP ANOTHER RECORD"
740  FOR F=1 TO 21
```

TEXAS INSTRUMENTS 99/4A

Add:
```
925  DATA 1 MIN 3.11 SEC
935  DATA BRITAIN,2 MIN 15.11 SEC
965  DATA USSR,4 MIN 22.8 SEC
975  DATA 7 MIN 23.22 SEC
985  DATA 3 MIN 42.22 SEC
1075 DATA E GERMANY,1 MIN 10.22 SEC
1085 DATA USSR,2 MIN 29.54 SEC
1115 DATA E GERMANY,4 MIN 36.29 SEC
1125 DATA 3 MIN 42.71 SEC
1135 DATA 4 MIN 6.67 SEC
```

Change:
```
100  CALL CLEAR
180  CALL CLEAR
```

(continued)

113

```
400 CALL CLEAR
740 FOR F=1 TO 28
920 DATA 100-M BREASTSTROKE,1976,JOHN HENCKEN,USA
930 DATA 200-M BREASTSTROKE,1976,DAVID WILLKIE
960 DATA 400-METER INDIV MED,1980,ALEKSANDR
    SIDORENKO
970 DATA 800-M FREESTYLE RELAY,1976,(TEAM),USA
980 DATA 400-M MEDLEY RELAY,1976,(TEAM),USA
1070 DATA 100-M BREASTSTROKE,1980,UTE GEWENIGER
1080 DATA 200-M BREASTSTROKE,1980,LINA KACHUSHITE
1110 DATA 400-M INDIV MEDLEY,1980,PETRA SCHNEIDER
1120 DATA 400-M FREESTYLE RELAY,1980,(TEAM),
     E GERMANY
1130 DATA 400-M MEDLEY RELAY,1980,(TEAM),E
     GERMANY
```

TRS-80 COLOR COMPUTER

Delete: 260, 320, 340, 780

Add: 305 IF E=7 THEN PRINT "HIT ENTER FOR REST OF LIST";
      306 IF E=7 THEN INPUT X$

Change: 100 CLS
         180 CLS
         220 PRINT "WOMEN'S OLYMPIC SWIMMING RECORDS";
         250 PRINT "MEN'S OLYMPIC SWIMMING RECORDS   ";
         300 PRINT E; TAB(5);R1$
         350 PRINT "TO SEE CURRENT OLYMPIC RECORD,"
         400 CLS
         440 PRINT "== MEN'S OLYMPIC RECORD BOOK =="
         560 PRINT "= WOMEN'S OLYMPIC RECORD BOOK ="
         740 FOR F=1 TO 31

Rowing Race

You can't row your boat gently down the stream if you expect to win an Olympic race. You have to be quick with the oars if you want to go for the gold. But watch out! Too many mistakes, and you'll get soaking wet!

☐ Sample Run

```
YOU ARE THE COXSWAIN OF A
FOUR-PERSON SHELL (A TYPE OF
BOAT) IN THE ROWING COMPETITION.

HERE'S YOUR SHELL:        Y---->
HERE'S THE OTHER SHELL: O---->

TO MOVE AHEAD, YOU HAVE TO
ENTER A WORD CORRECTLY.
FOUR WRONG WORDS AND YOU
MAY FALL IN THE WATER.

ENTER ANY KEY TO CONTINUE?


WWWWWWWWWWWWWWWWWWWWWWWWWWWWWWWWWW

Y---->

WWWWWWWWWWWWWWWWWWWWWWWWWWWWWWWWWW

O---->

WWWWWWWWWWWWWWWWWWWWWWWWWWWWWWWWWW


TO MOVE AHEAD,
TYPE IN THIS WORD:
PORT
? PORT


WWWWWWWWWWWWWWWWWWWWWWWWWWWWWWWWWW

   Y---->

WWWWWWWWWWWWWWWWWWWWWWWWWWWWWWWWWW

  O---->

WWWWWWWWWWWWWWWWWWWWWWWWWWWWWWWWWW
```

(continued)

```
TO MOVE AHEAD,
TYPE IN THIS WORD:
CROWD
? CROWD


WWWWWWWWWWWWWWWWWWWWWWWWWWWWWWWWWWWW

    Y---->

WWWWWWWWWWWWWWWWWWWWWWWWWWWWWWWWWWWW

  O---->

WWWWWWWWWWWWWWWWWWWWWWWWWWWWWWWWWWWW
```

[There's more — when you get to the end of the program, you'll see something like this:]

```
TO MOVE AHEAD,
TYPE IN THIS WORD:
PULL
? PULL


WWWWWWWWWWWWWWWWWWWWWWWWWWWWWWWWWWWW

                            Y---->

WWWWWWWWWWWWWWWWWWWWWWWWWWWWWWWWWWWW

                           O---->

WWWWWWWWWWWWWWWWWWWWWWWWWWWWWWWWWWWW


YOU WIN!
YOU'VE GOT A GOLD MEDAL CREW!
```

☐ Program Listing

```
10 REM ROWING RACE
100 Y$="Y---->"
110 O$="O---->"
120 PRINT "YOU ARE THE COXSWAIN OF A"
130 PRINT "FOUR-PERSON SHELL (A TYPE OF"
140 PRINT "BOAT) IN THE ROWING COMPETITION."
150 PRINT
160 PRINT "HERE'S YOUR SHELL:         ";Y$
170 PRINT "HERE'S THE OTHER SHELL: ";O$
180 PRINT
190 PRINT "TO MOVE AHEAD, YOU HAVE TO"
200 PRINT "ENTER A WORD CORRECTLY."
210 PRINT "FOUR WRONG WORDS AND YOU"
220 PRINT "MAY FALL IN THE WATER."
230 PRINT
240 PRINT "ENTER ANY KEY TO CONTINUE";
250 INPUT X$
260 YS=1
270 OS=1
280 FOR I=1 TO 1+INT(RND(1)*30)
290 READ R$
300 NEXT I
310 RESTORE
320 IF R$<>L$ THEN 340
330 GOTO 280
340 PRINT CHR$(12)
350 GOSUB 750
360 PRINT
370 PRINT
380 PRINT TAB(YS);Y$
390 PRINT
400 PRINT
410 GOSUB 750
420 PRINT
430 PRINT
440 PRINT TAB(OS);O$
450 PRINT
460 GOSUB 750
470 PRINT
480 PRINT
490 IF OS>30 OR YS>30 THEN 630
500 PRINT "TO MOVE AHEAD,"
510 PRINT "TYPE IN THIS WORD:"
520 PRINT R$
530 L$=R$
540 INPUT W$
550 IF W$="" THEN 500
560 IF INT(RND(1)*11)<10 THEN OS=OS+1
570 IF W$<>R$ THEN 600
580 YS=YS+1
590 GOTO 280
600 F=F+1
```

(continued)

```
610 IF F>3 THEN 690
620 GOTO 280
630 IF YS<31 THEN PRINT "YOU LOST!"
640 IF YS<31 THEN PRINT "YOU'LL SETTLE FOR SILVER."
650 IF YS>30 THEN PRINT "YOU WIN!"
660 IF YS>30 AND OS>30 THEN PRINT "BUT JUST BY A HAIR!"
670 IF YS>30 THEN PRINT "YOU'VE GOT A GOLD MEDAL CREW!"
680 END
690 IF INT(RND(1)*2)=1 THEN 280
700 PRINT
710 PRINT "S P L A S H !"
720 PRINT "LOOKS LIKE YOU'LL HAVE TO TRY AGAIN"
730 PRINT "IN FOUR YEARS!"
740 END
750 FOR I=1 TO 35
760 PRINT "W";
770 NEXT I
780 RETURN
790 DATA OARS,ROW,STROKE,PULL,KEEL
800 DATA BOW,STERN,SHELL,MEDAL,WATER
810 DATA SPEED,MEGAPHONE,YELL,ARMS,TIME
820 DATA HURRY,WAVES,WIND,PORT,STARBOARD
830 DATA RUDDER,BOAT,GOLD,SILVER,BRONZE
840 DATA CROWD,LANE,CHEER,RACE,FIRST
```

☐ If You Have . . .

APPLE II

Change: 340 HOME

ATARI

Add: 95 DIM Y$(6),O$(6),X$(1),R$(11),L$(11),W$(11)
```
855 FOR A=1 TO IDX
865 PRINT " ";:NEXT A:RETURN
```

Change: 280 FOR I=1 TO 1+INT(RND(0)*30)
```
340 PRINT CHR$(125)
380 IDX=YS:GOSUB 855:PRINT Y$
440 IDX=OS:GOSUB 855:PRINT O$
560 IF INT(RND(0)*11)<10 THEN OS=OS+1
690 IF INT(RND(0)*2)=1 THEN 280
```

COMMODORE 64

Change: 340 PRINT CHR$(147)

COMMODORE VIC-20

```
Change:   340  PRINT CHR$(147)
          490  IF OS>15 OR YS>15 THEN 630
          630  IF YS<16 THEN PRINT "YOU LOST!"
          640  IF YS<16 THEN PRINT "YOU'LL SETTLE FOR SILVER."
          650  IF YS>15 THEN PRINT "YOU WIN!"
          660  IF YS>15 AND OS>15 THEN PRINT "BUT JUST BY A
               HAIR!"
          670  IF YS>15 THEN PRINT "YOU'VE GOT A GOLD MEDAL
               CREW!"
          750  FOR I=1 TO 21
```

TEXAS INSTRUMENTS 99/4A

```
Add:      565  OS=OS+1
          645  PRINT "YOU'LL SETTLE FOR SILVER"
          652  PRINT "YOU WIN!"
          653  IF OS<=23 THEN 670

Change:   280  FOR I=1 TO 1+INT(RND*30)
          340  CALL CLEAR
          490  IF (OS>23)+(YS>23) THEN 630
          560  IF INT(RND*11)>=10 THEN 570
          630  IF YS>=23 THEN 650
          640  PRINT "YOU LOST!"
          650  IF YS<=23 THEN 680
          660  PRINT "BUT JUST BY A HAIR!"
          670  PRINT "YOU'VE GOT A GOLD MEDAL CREW!"
          690  IF INT(RND*2)=1 THEN 280
          750  FOR I=1 TO 28
```

TRS-80 COLOR COMPUTER

```
Change:   280  FOR I=1 TO RND(30)
          340  CLS
          490  IF OS>25 OR YS>25 THEN 630
          560  IF RND(11)<10 THEN OS=OS+1
          630  IF YS<26 THEN PRINT "YOU LOST!"
          640  IF YS<26 THEN PRINT "YOU'LL HAVE TO SETTLE
               FOR SILVER."
          650  IF YS>25 THEN PRINT "YOU WIN!"
          660  IF YS>25 AND OS>25 THEN PRINT "BUT JUST BY A
               HAIR!"
          670  IF YS>25 THEN PRINT "YOU'VE GOT A GOLD MEDAL
               CREW!"
          690  IF RND(2)=1 THEN 280
          750  FOR I=1 TO 31
```

International Olympic Months

Around the world, athletes train for months on end to get into the Olympic Games. But exactly what are those months called in foreign countries? This program gives you the answers in five languages!

☐ Sample Run

```
WHAT'S THE NAME OF THE MONTH
IN YOUR OPPONENT'S LANGUAGE?
THIS PROGRAM WILL HELP YOU FIND OUT.

   1   ENGLISH
   2   SWEDISH
   3   FRENCH
   4   ITALIAN
   5   SPANISH
   6   GERMAN

SELECT A LANGUAGE BY NUMBER? 2

LANGUAGE SELECTED: SWEDISH

   1   JANUARY
   2   FEBRUARY
   3   MARCH
   4   APRIL
   5   MAY
   6   JUNE
   7   JULY
   8   AUGUST
   9   SEPTEMBER
  10   OCTOBER
  11   NOVEMBER
  12   DECEMBER

(TO SWITCH LANGUAGES, ENTER "S"
--TO QUIT, ENTER "Q")
TO TRANSLATE A MONTH,
ENTER THE CORRECT NUMBER? 10

IN SWEDISH, OCTOBER IS OKTOBER.
```

[There's more — when you get to the end of the program, you'll see something like this:]

```
IN ITALIAN, FEBRUARY IS FEBBRAIO.

    1    JANUARY
    2    FEBRUARY
    3    MARCH
    4    APRIL
    5    MAY
    6    JUNE
    7    JULY
    8    AUGUST
    9    SEPTEMBER
    10   OCTOBER
    11   NOVEMBER
    12   DECEMBER

(TO SWITCH LANGUAGES, ENTER "S"
--TO QUIT, ENTER "Q")
TO TRANSLATE A MONTH,
ENTER THE CORRECT NUMBER? Q
```

☐ Program Listing

```
10 REM INTERNATIONAL OLYMPIC MONTHS
100 PRINT
110 PRINT "WHAT'S THE NAME OF THE MONTH"
120 PRINT "IN YOUR OPPONENT'S LANGUAGE?"
130 PRINT "THIS PROGRAM WILL HELP YOU FIND OUT."
140 PRINT
150 PRINT
160 FOR C=1 TO 6
170 Y=C
180 GOSUB 680
190 PRINT TAB(2);C;TAB(5);F$
200 NEXT C
210 PRINT
220 PRINT "SELECT A LANGUAGE BY NUMBER";
230 INPUT L$
240 L=VAL(L$)
250 IF L<1 OR L>6 THEN 220
260 Y=L
270 GOSUB 680
280 PRINT
290 PRINT "LANGUAGE SELECTED: ";F$
300 PRINT
```

(continued)

```
310 FOR D=1 TO 12
320 Y=6
330 Z=(D*6)-5
340 GOSUB 680
350 PRINT TAB(2);D;TAB(7);M$
360 NEXT D
370 PRINT
380 PRINT "(TO SWITCH LANGUAGES, ENTER ";CHR$(34);"S";
    CHR$(34)
390 PRINT "--TO QUIT, ENTER ";CHR$(34);"Q";CHR$(34);")"
400 PRINT "TO TRANSLATE A MONTH,"
410 PRINT "ENTER THE CORRECT NUMBER";
420 INPUT C$
430 IF C$="Q" THEN END
440 C=VAL(C$)
450 IF C$="S" THEN 150
460 IF C>0 AND C<13 THEN 480
470 GOTO 410
480 PRINT
490 PRINT
500 Y=L
510 GOSUB 680
520 PRINT "IN ";F$;", ";
530 Y=6
540 Z=(C*6)-5
550 GOSUB 680
560 PRINT M$;" IS ";
570 T$=M$
580 Z=(C*6)-(6-L)
590 GOSUB 680
600 PRINT M$;"."
610 PRINT
620 IF M$<>T$ THEN 300
630 Y=L
640 GOSUB 680
650 PRINT "SEE? YOU ALREADY KNOW A LITTLE ";F$;"!"
660 GOTO 300
670 REM --- READING SUBROUTINE ---
680 FOR P=1 TO Y
690 READ F$
700 NEXT P
710 FOR Q=1 TO Z
720 READ M$
730 NEXT Q
740 RESTORE
750 RETURN
760 DATA ENGLISH,SWEDISH,FRENCH,ITALIAN,SPANISH,GERMAN
770 DATA JANUARY,JANUARI,JANVIER,GENNAIO,ENERO,JANUAR
780 DATA FEBRUARY,FEBRUARI,FEVRIER,FEBBRAIO,FEBRERO,
    FEBRUAR
790 DATA MARCH,MARS,MARS,MARZO,MARZO,MARZ
800 DATA APRIL,APRIL,AVRIL,APRILE,ABRIL,APRIL
810 DATA MAY,MAJ,MAI,MAGGIO,MAYO,MAI
820 DATA JUNE,JUNI,JUIN,GIUGNO,JUNIO,JUNI
830 DATA JULY,JULI,JUILLET,LUGLIO,JULIO,JULI
```

```
840 DATA AUGUST,AUGUSTI,AOUT,AGOSTO,AGOSTO,AUGUST
850 DATA SEPTEMBER,SEPTEMBER,SEPTEMBRE,SETTEMBRE,
    SEPTIEMBRE,SEPTEMBER
860 DATA OCTOBER,OKTOBER,OCTOBRE,OTTOBRE,OCTUBRE,OKTOBER
870 DATA NOVEMBER,NOVEMBER,NOVEMBRE,NOBEMBRE,NOVIEMBRE,
    NOVEMBER
880 DATA DECEMBER,DECEMBER,DECEMBRE,DICEMBRE,DICIEMBRE,
    DEZEMBER
```

☐ If You Have . . .

APPLE II   No Changes Required

ATARI

Add:
```
95 DIM F$(11),L$(2),M$(11),C$(2),T$(11)
351 IDX=3:IF D>=10 THEN IDX=2
352 GOSUB 895:PRINT M$
895 FOR A=1 TO IDX
905 PRINT " ";:NEXT A:RETURN
```

Change:
```
190 IDX=2:GOSUB 895:PRINT C;:GOSUB 895:PRINT F$
350 IDX=2:GOSUB 895:PRINT D;
440 IF C$="S" THEN 150
450 IF ASC(C$)<49 OR ASC(C$)>57 THEN 410
460 C=VAL(C$):GOTO 480
```

COMMODORE 64   No Changes Required

COMMODORE VIC-20

Change:
```
220 PRINT "SELECT A LANGUAGE BY NUMBER"
410 PRINT "ENTER THE CORRECT NUMBER"
```

TEXAS INSTRUMENTS 99/4A

Add:
```
890 END
465 GOTO 480
```

Change:
```
250 IF (L<1)+(L>6) THEN 220
430 IF C$="Q" THEN 890
440 IF C$="S" THEN 150
450 IF (ASC(C$)<49)+(ASC(C$)>57) THEN 410
460 C=VAL(C$)
```

TRS-80 COLOR COMPUTER

Delete: 370

Fix the Scoreboard!

At the Montreal Olympics in 1976, Romania's Nadia Comaneci gave the scoreboard computer nothing but trouble. For the first time in the history of the Games, a gymnast received perfect 10 scores — but the computer was programmed to go no higher than 9.9! Even your home computer can do better than that. But there still seem to be a few bugs in the Olympic scoreboard. See if you have what it takes to fix them!

☐ Sample Run

```
HOW MANY DAYS HAS IT BEEN
SINCE THE START OF THE OLYMPICS? 5

YOU'RE IN CHARGE OF THE SCOREBOARD,
BUT IT'S OUT OF ORDER.

NMMMB
TGLBPQUU
KRVRYTHTREZFJ
SGXMXLUUSIMXCWTOFIAJIFUEWJFOJSRJPSCHIU

THE WORST PART IS THAT
IT'S SCRAMBLING THE NAMES
OF THE COUNTRIES.

HERE'S A SCRAMBLED ONE NOW:
ACUB

QUICK! BEFORE THE CROWD NOTICES!
UNSCRAMBLE THAT COUNTRY!
? CUBA

RIGHT!
BUT THERE'S ANOTHER PROBLEM:
OYSVAUIALG

QUICK! BEFORE THE CROWD NOTICES!
UNSCRAMBLE THAT COUNTRY!
? ALVOSLAGIE
NO!
HURRY!
TRY AGAIN!
THE LAST LETTER OF THE COUNTRY IS A
OYSVAUIALG

QUICK! BEFORE THE CROWD NOTICES!
UNSCRAMBLE THAT COUNTRY!
? SYOVALAGU
NO!
```

```
ONE MORE CHANCE!
TRY AGAIN!
THE LAST 2 LETTERS OF THE COUNTRY ARE IA
OYSVAUIALG

QUICK! BEFORE THE CROWD NOTICES!
UNSCRAMBLE THAT COUNTRY!
? YUGOSLAVIA
```

[There's more—when you get to the end of the program, you'll see something like this:]

```
RIGHT!
BUT THERE'S ANOTHER PROBLEM:
AJNAP

QUICK! BEFORE THE CROWD NOTICES!
UNSCRAMBLE THAT COUNTRY!
? JAPAN

RIGHT!
YOU'VE DONE IT!
YOU'VE FIXED THE SCOREBOARD!
THE CROWD GIVES YOU A STANDING OVATION!
```

☐ Program Listing

```
10 REM FIX THE SCOREBOARD!
100 PRINT "HOW MANY DAYS HAS IT BEEN"
110 PRINT "SINCE THE START OF THE OLYMPICS";
120 INPUT S
130 RANDOMIZE S
140 PRINT
150 DIM C(20),A(6)
160 PRINT "YOU'RE IN CHARGE OF THE SCOREBOARD,"
170 PRINT "BUT IT'S OUT OF ORDER."
180 PRINT
190 FOR I=1 TO 20
200 C(I)=1+INT(RND(1)*20)
210 PRINT CHR$(65+RND(1)*26);
220 FOR J=I-1 TO 1 STEP -1
230 IF C(I)=C(J) THEN 200
240 NEXT J
250 IF I/5=INT(I/5) THEN PRINT
260 NEXT I
270 PRINT
280 PRINT "THE WORST PART IS THAT"
290 PRINT "IT'S SCRAMBLING THE NAMES"
300 PRINT "OF THE COUNTRIES."
310 PRINT
```

(continued)

```
320 PRINT "HERE'S A SCRAMBLED ONE NOW:"
330 R=1+INT(RND(1)*20)
340 FOR B=1 TO W
350 IF R=A(B) THEN 330
360 NEXT B
370 FOR I=1 TO R
380 READ C$
390 NEXT I
400 RESTORE
410 FOR I=1 TO 20
420 IF C(I)<LEN(C$)+1 THEN PRINT MID$(C$,C(I),1);
430 NEXT I
440 PRINT
450 PRINT
460 PRINT "QUICK! BEFORE THE CROWD NOTICES!"
470 PRINT "UNSCRAMBLE THAT COUNTRY!"
480 INPUT A$
490 IF A$="" THEN 460
500 IF A$=C$ THEN 680
510 PRINT "NO!"
520 IF F=0 THEN PRINT "HURRY!"
530 IF F=1 THEN PRINT "ONE MORE CHANCE!"
540 IF F=2 THEN 640
550 PRINT "TRY AGAIN!"
560 F=F+1
570 IF F=2 THEN 610
580 PRINT "THE LAST LETTER OF THE COUNTRY IS ";
590 PRINT MID$(C$,LEN(C$),1)
600 GOTO 630
610 PRINT "THE LAST 2 LETTERS OF THE COUNTRY ARE ";
620 PRINT MID$(C$,LEN(C$)-1,2)
630 GOTO 410
640 PRINT
650 PRINT "THE COUNTRY IS "; C$; "!"
660 PRINT "TAKE A LONG SHOWER AND DON'T COME BACK!"
670 END
680 PRINT
690 PRINT "RIGHT!"
700 F=0
710 IF W=5 THEN 760
720 PRINT "BUT THERE'S ANOTHER PROBLEM:"
730 W=W+1
740 A(W)=R
750 GOTO 330
760 PRINT "YOU'VE DONE IT!"
770 PRINT "YOU'VE FIXED THE SCOREBOARD!"
780 PRINT "THE CROWD GIVES YOU A STANDING OVATION!"
790 DATA UNITED STATES,U.S.S.R.,EAST GERMANY
800 DATA WEST GERMANY,JAPAN,POLAND,BULGARIA
810 DATA CUBA,ROMANIA,HUNGARY,FINLAND
820 DATA SWEDEN,ENGLAND,ITALY,CZECHOSLOVAKIA
830 DATA FRANCE,YUGOSLAVIA,NEW ZEALAND
840 DATA SOUTH KOREA,SWITZERLAND
```

☐ If You Have . . .

APPLE II

Delete: 130

ATARI

Delete: 130

```
Add:    95 DIM C$(20),A$(20)
```

```
Change: 200 C(I)=1+INT(RND(0)*20)
        210 PRINT CHR$(65+RND(0)*26);
        330 R=1+INT(RND(0)*20)
        420 IF C(I)<LEN(C$)+1 THEN PRINT C$(C(I),C(I));
        590 PRINT C$(LEN(C$),LEN(C$))
        620 PRINT C$(LEN(C$)-1,LEN(C$))
```

COMMODORE 64

Delete: 130

```
Change: 200 C(I)=1+INT(RND(0)*20)
        210 PRINT CHR$(65+RND(0)*26);
        330 R=1+INT(RND(0)*20)
```

COMMODORE VIC-20

Delete: 130

```
Change: 110 PRINT "SINCE THE START OF THE OLYMPICS"
        200 C(I)=1+INT(RND(0)*20)
        210 PRINT CHR$(65+RND(0)*26);
        330 R=1+INT(RND(0)*20)
```

TEXAS INSTRUMENTS 99/4A

```
Add:    255 PRINT
        425 PRINT SEG$(C$,C(I),1);
        525 PRINT "HURRY!"
        535 PRINT "ONE MORE CHANCE!"
```

```
Change: 200 C(I)=1+INT(RND*20);
        210 PRINT CHR$(65+RND*26);
        250 IF I/5<>INT(I/5) THEN 260
        330 R=1+INT(RND*20)
        420 IF C(I)>=LEN(C$)+1 THEN 430
        520 IF F<>0 THEN 530
```

(continued)

```
530 IF F<>1 THEN 540
590 PRINT SEG$(C$,LEN(C$),1)
620 PRINT SEG$(C$,LEN(C$)-1,2)
```

TRS-80 COLOR COMPUTER

Delete: 130

Change: 200 C(I)=RND(20)
         210 PRINT CHR$(64+RND(26));
         330 R=RND(20)

Soccer Finals

It's down to the last precious seconds. Make a goal and your team wins —
if not, you'll send the game into overtime. If you have a golden foot,
you'll win your team a gold medal!

☐ Sample Run

```
YOU'RE THE STAR
OF THE AMERICAN SOCCER TEAM.

IT'S THE FINAL GAME,
AND THE SCORE IS TIED
WITH ONLY SECONDS TO GO.

AN OPPOSING FORWARD
SHOVES YOU AS YOU MOVE TOWARD
HIS GOAL!

IF YOU MAKE THIS PENALTY KICK
YOU'LL WIN THE GOLD MEDAL FOR YOUR TEAM!

THE OPPOSING GOALKEEPER STARES AT YOU,
DARING YOU TO PUT THE BALL PAST HIM.

HOW MANY SECONDS ARE LEFT? 3

WHICH WAY WILL YOU KICK THE BALL?

    1   TO THE GOALKEEPER'S LEFT
    2   STRAIGHT AT THE GOALKEEPER
    3   TO THE GOALKEEPER'S RIGHT

WHICH WAY? 3

HOW HIGH WILL YOU KICK THE BALL?

    1   ALONG THE GROUND
    2   AT WAIST HEIGHT
    3   TOWARD THE TOP OF THE GOAL

HOW HIGH? 3

THE GOALKEEPER MOVES LEFT
AND DIVES TOWARD THE GROUND.
THE BALL HURTLES
TOWARD THE GOALKEEPER'S RIGHT
AND SAILS ABOVE HIS HEAD!
```

(continued)

```
GOAL!
THE CROWD GOES WILD!
THEY HAIL YOU AS THE HERO!

HOW MANY SECONDS ARE LEFT? 3

WHICH WAY WILL YOU KICK THE BALL?

   1   TO THE GOALKEEPER'S LEFT
   2   STRAIGHT AT THE GOALKEEPER
   3   TO THE GOALKEEPER'S RIGHT

WHICH WAY? 1

HOW HIGH WILL YOU KICK THE BALL?

   1   ALONG THE GROUND
   2   AT WAIST HEIGHT
   3   TOWARD THE TOP OF THE GOAL

HOW HIGH? 1

THE GOALKEEPER MOVES LEFT
AND DIVES TOWARD THE GROUND.
IT LOOKS LIKE HE HAS IT!
HE DOES!
THE GOALKEEPER'S GOT IT!
THE CLOCK RUNS OUT!
YOU'LL HAVE TO PLAY A TIEBREAKER!
```

☐ Program Listing

```
10 REM SOCCER FINALS
100 PRINT
110 PRINT "YOU'RE THE STAR"
120 PRINT "OF THE AMERICAN SOCCER TEAM."
130 PRINT
140 PRINT "IT'S THE FINAL GAME,"
150 PRINT "AND THE SCORE IS TIED"
160 PRINT "WITH ONLY SECONDS TO GO."
170 PRINT
180 PRINT "AN OPPOSING FORWARD"
190 PRINT "SHOVES YOU AS YOU MOVE TOWARD"
200 PRINT "HIS GOAL!"
210 PRINT
220 PRINT "IF YOU MAKE THIS PENALTY KICK"
230 PRINT "YOU'LL WIN THE GOLD MEDAL FOR YOUR TEAM!"
240 PRINT
250 PRINT "THE OPPOSING GOALKEEPER STARES AT YOU,"
```

```
260 PRINT "DARING YOU TO PUT THE BALL PAST HIM."
270 PRINT
280 PRINT "HOW MANY SECONDS ARE LEFT";
290 INPUT N
300 RANDOMIZE N
310 PRINT
320 R=1+INT(RND(1)*3)
330 U=1+INT(RND(1)*3)
340 PRINT "WHICH WAY WILL YOU KICK THE BALL?"
350 PRINT
360 PRINT " 1   TO THE GOALKEEPER'S LEFT"
370 PRINT " 2   STRAIGHT AT THE GOALKEEPER"
380 PRINT " 3   TO THE GOALKEEPER'S RIGHT"
390 PRINT
400 PRINT "WHICH WAY";
410 INPUT W
420 IF W<1 OR W>3 THEN 400
430 PRINT
440 PRINT "HOW HIGH WILL YOU KICK THE BALL?"
450 PRINT
460 PRINT " 1   ALONG THE GROUND"
470 PRINT " 2   AT WAIST HEIGHT"
480 PRINT " 3   TOWARD THE TOP OF THE GOAL"
490 PRINT
500 PRINT "HOW HIGH";
510 INPUT H
520 PRINT
530 IF H<1 OR H>3 THEN 500
540 K=1+INT(RND(1)*10)
550 PRINT "THE GOALKEEPER MOVES ";
560 GOSUB 610
570 PRINT "AND ";
580 GOSUB 660
590 IF W=R AND U=H THEN 710
600 GOTO 810
610 IF R=1 THEN PRINT "LEFT"
620 IF R=2 THEN PRINT "FORWARD"
630 IF R=3 THEN PRINT "RIGHT"
640 GOSUB 1070
650 RETURN
660 IF U=1 THEN PRINT "DIVES TOWARD THE GROUND."
670 IF U=2 THEN PRINT "REACHES FOR THE BALL."
680 IF U=3 THEN PRINT "JUMPS INTO THE AIR."
690 GOSUB 1070
700 RETURN
710 PRINT "IT LOOKS LIKE HE HAS IT!"
720 IF Z<9 THEN 790
730 GOSUB 1070
740 PRINT "NO!  THE BALL SPINS";
750 IF H>2 THEN PRINT " OVER HIS HEAD ";
760 IF U=H THEN PRINT " AROUND HIM ";
770 PRINT "INTO THE GOAL!"
780 GOTO 1020
790 PRINT "HE DOES!"
800 GOTO 970
```

(continued)

```
810 PRINT "THE BALL HURTLES"
820 IF W-R>0 THEN PRINT "TOWARD THE GOALKEEPER'S RIGHT"
830 IF W-R<0 THEN PRINT "TOWARD THE GOALKEEPER'S LEFT"
840 IF R-W=0 THEN PRINT "STRAIGHT TOWARD THE GOALKEEPER"
850 GOSUB 1070
860 IF H-U>0 THEN PRINT "AND SAILS ABOVE HIS HEAD!"
870 IF H-U<0 THEN PRINT "AND DOWN TOWARD HIS KNEES!"
880 IF H=U THEN PRINT "LIKE A SHOT!"
890 IF H=U OR W=R THEN 930
900 IF ABS(H-U)=1 OR ABS(W-R)=1 THEN 950
910 IF K<3 THEN 970
920 GOTO 1020
930 IF K<7 THEN 970
940 GOTO 1020
950 IF K<5 THEN 970
960 GOTO 1020
970 GOSUB 1070
980 PRINT "THE GOALKEEPER'S GOT IT!"
990 PRINT "THE CLOCK RUNS OUT!"
1000 PRINT "YOU'LL HAVE TO PLAY A TIEBREAKER!"
1010 END
1020 PRINT
1030 PRINT "GOAL!"
1040 PRINT "THE CROWD GOES WILD!"
1050 PRINT "THEY HAIL YOU AS THE HERO!"
1060 END
1070 FOR I=1 TO 400
1080 NEXT I
1090 RETURN
```

☐ If You Have . . .

APPLE II

Delete: 300

ATARI

Delete: 300

```
Change:  320 R=1+INT(RND(0)*3)
         330 U=1+INT(RND(0)*3)
         540 K=1+INT(RND(0)*10)
```

COMMODORE 64

Delete: 300

Change: 320 R=1+INT(RND(0)*3)
        330 U=1+INT(RND(0)*3)
        540 K=1+INT(RND(0)*10)

COMMODORE VIC-20

Delete: 130, 170, 210, 240, 300

Change: 280 PRINT "HOW MANY SECONDS ARE LEFT"
        320 R=1+INT(RND(0)*3)
        330 U=1+INT(RND(0)*3)
        400 PRINT "WHICH WAY"
        500 PRINT "HOW HIGH"
        540 K=1+INT(RND(0)*10)

TEXAS INSTRUMENTS 99/4A

Add: 615 PRINT "LEFT"
     625 PRINT "FORWARD"
     635 PRINT "RIGHT"
     665 PRINT "DIVES TOWARD THE GROUND."
     675 PRINT "REACHES FOR THE BALL."
     685 PRINT "JUMPS INTO THE AIR."
     755 PRINT " OVER HIS HEAD ";
     765 PRINT " AROUND HIM ";
     825 PRINT "TOWARD THE GOALKEEPER'S RIGHT"
     835 PRINT "TOWARD THE GOALKEEPER'S LEFT"
     845 PRINT "STRAIGHT TOWARD THE GOALKEEPER"
     865 PRINT "AND SAILS ABOVE HIS HEAD!"
     875 PRINT "AND DOWN TOWARD HIS KNEES!"
     885 PRINT "LIKE A SHOT!"

Change: 320 R=1+INT(RND*3)
        330 U=1+INT(RND*3)
        420 IF (W<1)+(W>3) THEN 400
        530 IF (H<1)+(H>3) THEN 500
        540 K=1+INT(RND*10)
        590 IF (W=R)*(U=H) THEN 710
        610 IF R<>1 THEN 620
        620 IF R<>2 THEN 630
        630 IF R<>3 THEN 640
        660 IF U<>1 THEN 670
        670 IF U<>2 THEN 680
        680 IF U<>3 THEN 690
        750 IF H<=2 THEN 760
        760 IF U<>H THEN 770
        820 IF W-R<=0 THEN 830
        830 IF W-R>=0 THEN 840
        840 IF R-W<>0 THEN 850
        860 IF H-U<=0 THEN 870
        870 IF H-U>=0 THEN 880
        880 IF H<>U THEN 890

(continued)

```
890 IF (H=U)+(W=R) THEN 930
900 IF (ABS(H-U)=1)+(ABS(W-R)=1) THEN 950
```

TRS-80 COLOR COMPUTER

Delete: 130, 170, 210, 240, 300

Change: 250 PRINT "THE OPPOSING GOALKEEPER STARES AT YOU, ";
        320 R=RND(3)
        330 U=RND(3)
        540 K=RND(10)

Archery Range

In official Olympic competition, archers shoot 144 arrows in four days. In this computer competition, you'll get one day's worth of shooting — 36 arrows. When you're all through, your score will be multiplied by four to give you a total you can compare with the official Olympic records. Aim well!

☐ Sample Run

```
HOW GOOD AN ARCHER ARE YOU?

YOU GET 36 SHOTS:
9 FROM EACH OF 4 DISTANCES
STARTING AT 30 METERS
AND INCREASING BY 20 METERS
EACH ROUND.

YOU'LL SEE YOUR ARROW FLY
ACROSS THE SCREEN.
THEN YOU'LL BE ABLE TO CHECK
THE TARGET.  THE MISSING NUMBER
IS THE ONE YOU JUST HIT!

HIT THE ENTER KEY TO BEGIN?
2   4   6   8   10   8   6   4   2

YOU HAVE 9 ARROWS LEFT
AT A DISTANCE OF 30 METERS.

45 TO 48 POUNDS OF PULL IS IDEAL:
HOW MANY POUNDS OF PULL DO YOU WANT? 47

>------->

        >------->

            >------->

                >------->

                    >------->

    2    4   6   8        8   6   4   2

YOU NOW HAVE A TOTAL OF 10 POINTS.

YOU HAVE 8 ARROWS LEFT
AT A DISTANCE OF 30 METERS.
```

(continued)

```
45 TO 48 POUNDS OF PULL IS IDEAL:
HOW MANY POUNDS OF PULL DO YOU WANT? 46

>------>
        >------>
                >------>
                        >------>
                                >------>
 2   4   6   8   10   8     4   2

YOU NOW HAVE A TOTAL OF 16 POINTS.
```

*[There's more — when you get to the end of the program, you'll see
something like this:]*

```
YOU NOW HAVE A TOTAL OF 64 POINTS.

YOU HAVE 1 ARROW LEFT
AT A DISTANCE OF 30 METERS.

45 TO 48 POUNDS OF PULL IS IDEAL:
HOW MANY POUNDS OF PULL DO YOU WANT? 47

>------>
        >------>
                >------>
                        >------>
                                >------>
 2   4   6   8       8   6   4   2

YOU NOW HAVE A TOTAL OF 74 POINTS.

YOUR FINAL POINT TOTAL IS: 320

THAT'S EQUIVALENT TO
AN OLYMPIC TOTAL OF 2560 POINTS.
```

□ Program Listing

```
10 REM ARCHERY RANGE
100 PRINT
110 PRINT "HOW GOOD AN ARCHER ARE YOU?"
120 M=30
130 PRINT
140 PRINT "YOU GET 36 SHOTS:"
150 PRINT "9 FROM EACH OF 4 DISTANCES"
160 PRINT "STARTING AT 30 METERS"
170 PRINT "AND INCREASING BY 20 METERS"
180 PRINT "EACH ROUND."
190 PRINT
200 PRINT "YOU'LL SEE YOUR ARROW FLY"
210 PRINT "ACROSS THE SCREEN."
220 PRINT "THEN YOU'LL BE ABLE TO CHECK"
230 PRINT "THE TARGET.  THE MISSING NUMBER"
240 PRINT "IS THE ONE YOU JUST HIT!"
250 PRINT
260 PRINT "HIT THE ENTER KEY TO BEGIN";
270 INPUT X$
280 PRINT CHR$(12)
290 GOSUB 700
300 PRINT
310 PRINT
320 D=30
330 FOR R=1 TO 9
340 PRINT "YOU HAVE ";10-R;" ARROWS LEFT"
350 PRINT "AT A DISTANCE OF ";D;" METERS."
360 PRINT
370 PRINT "45 TO 48 POUNDS OF PULL IS IDEAL:"
380 PRINT "HOW MANY POUNDS OF PULL DO YOU WANT";
390 INPUT S
400 IF S=0 THEN 370
410 J=18-(RND(1)*13)-(D/10*INT(RND(ABS(S-44))))-(D/S)
420 L=INT(RND(1)*2)
430 IF S<45 OR S>48 THEN J=J-ABS(S-45)
440 GOSUB 940
450 PRINT CHR$(7)
460 GOSUB 650
470 P=P+J
480 PRINT
490 PRINT
500 PRINT "YOU NOW HAVE A TOTAL OF";P;"POINTS."
510 PRINT
520 NEXT R
530 D=D+20
540 IF D>90 THEN 590
550 PRINT
560 PRINT "NEW ROUND!  THE DISTANCE GOES UP TO"
570 PRINT D;" METERS."
580 PRINT
590 IF D<91 THEN 330
600 PRINT "YOUR FINAL POINT TOTAL IS: ";P          (continued)
```

```
610  PRINT
620  PRINT "THAT'S EQUIVALENT TO"
630  PRINT "AN OLYMPIC TOTAL OF ";P*8; " POINTS."
640  END
650  IF J<2 THEN J=0
660  IF J=0 THEN PRINT
670  IF J=0 THEN L=0
680  PRINT CHR$(12)
690  IF J=0 THEN PRINT "MISSED THE TARGET!"
700  FOR I=2 TO 8 STEP 2
710  IF F=1 OR L<>1 OR J>I THEN 760
720  PRINT "    ";
730  J=I
740  F=1
750  GOTO 770
760  PRINT I; " ";
770  NEXT I
780  IF J>8 THEN J=10
790  IF J<10 THEN PRINT " 10   ";
800  IF J>8 THEN J=10
810  IF J=10 THEN PRINT "       ";
820  IF J=10 THEN F=1
830  FOR I=8 TO 2 STEP -2
840  IF F=1 OR L=1 OR J<I THEN 890
850  PRINT "    ";
860  J=I
870  F=1
880  GOTO 900
890  PRINT I; " ";
900  NEXT I
910  F=0
920  L=0
930  RETURN
940  FOR I=1 TO 25
950  PRINT TAB(I);">------>"
960  NEXT I
970  RETURN
```

☐ If You Have . . .

APPLE II

Change: 260 PRINT "HIT THE RETURN KEY TO BEGIN";
         280 HOME
         500 PRINT "YOU NOW HAVE A TOTAL OF ";P;" POINTS."
         680 HOME

ATARI

```
Add:   95 DIM X$(1)
      985 FOR A=1 TO IDX
      995 PRINT " ";:NEXT A:RETURN

Change: 260 PRINT "HIT THE RETURN KEY TO BEGIN";
        280 PRINT CHR$(125)
        410 J=18-(RND(0)*13)-(D/10*INT(RND(ABS(S-44))))-(D/S)
        420 L=INT(RND(0)*2)
        500 PRINT "YOU NOW HAVE A TOTAL OF ";P;" POINTS."
        680 PRINT CHR$(125)
        950 IDX=I:GOSUB 985:PRINT ">------>"
```

COMMODORE 64

```
Change: 260 PRINT "HIT THE RETURN KEY TO BEGIN";
        280 PRINT CHR$(147)
        680 PRINT CHR$(147)
```

COMMODORE VIC-20

```
Delete: 190

Change: 260 PRINT "HIT THE RETURN KEY TO BEGIN"
        280 PRINT CHR$(147)
        380 PRINT "HOW MANY POUNDS OF PULL DO YOU WANT"
        680 PRINT CHR$(147)
        940 FOR I=1 TO 14
```

TEXAS INSTRUMENTS 99/4A

```
Add:   435 J=J-ABS(S-45)
       655 J=0
       665 PRINT
       695 PRINT "MISSED THE TARGET!"
       785 J=10
       795 PRINT " 10   "
       805 J=10
       815 PRINT "        ";

Change: 280 CALL CLEAR
        410 J=18-(RND*13)-(D/10*INT(RND(ABS(S-44))))-(D/S)
        420 L=INT(RND*2)
        430 IF (S>44)*(S<49) THEN 440
        450 CALL SOUND (100,440,2)
        650 IF J>=2 THEN 660
        660 IF J<>0 THEN 680
        670 L=0
        680 CALL CLEAR
        690 IF J<>0 THEN 700
```

(continued)

```
710 IF (F=1)+(L<>1)+(J>1) THEN 760
780 IF J<=8 THEN 790
790 IF J>=10 THEN 800
800 IF J<=8 THEN 810
810 IF J<>10 THEN 830
820 F=1
840 IF (F=1)+(L=1)+(J<1) THEN 890
940 FOR I=1 TO 21
```

TRS-80 COLOR COMPUTER

Delete: 130

Change: 280 CLS
```
410 J=19-RND(13)-(D/10*RND(ABS(S-44)))-D/S
420 L=RND(2)
450 SOUND 173,3
680 CLS
760 PRINT I;
890 PRINT I;
940 FOR I=1 TO 23
```

Athlete Speedometer

The record holder in the 100-meter dash is often called "The World's Fastest Human." But how fast did he go? And how fast are other athletes going when they run or swim? Here's the speedometer that will tell you!

☐ Sample Run

```
HOW FAST IS THAT SPEEDY OLYMPIC
ATHLETE?  I'LL LET YOU FIGURE IT
OUT PRECISELY.

HOW IS THE RACE MEASURED:
METERS, KILOMETERS, YARDS, OR MILES? METERS

HOW MANY METERS IS THE RACE? 100

USE COLONS AND DECIMAL POINT
TO SEPARATE THE TIME:
(3:45:20.2--NOT
3 HOURS,45 MINUTES,20.2 SECONDS)

WHAT IS THE ATHLETE'S TIME? 9.9

THE ATHLETE'S SPEED IS:
 36.36364  KILOMETERS PER HOUR
 22.60015  MILES PER HOUR

RUN

HOW FAST IS THAT SPEEDY OLYMPIC
ATHLETE?  I'LL LET YOU FIGURE IT
OUT PRECISELY.

HOW IS THE RACE MEASURED:
METERS, KILOMETERS, YARDS, OR MILES? KILOMETERS

HOW MANY KILOMETERS IS THE RACE? 10

USE COLONS AND DECIMAL POINT
TO SEPARATE THE TIME:
(3:45:20.2--NOT
3 HOURS,45 MINUTES,20.2 SECONDS)

WHAT IS THE ATHLETE'S TIME? 27:40.38

THE ATHLETE'S SPEED IS:
 21.68283  KILOMETERS PER HOUR
 13.47597  MILES PER HOUR
```

□ Program Listing

```
10 REM ATHLETE SPEEDOMETER
100 PRINT
110 PRINT "HOW FAST IS THAT SPEEDY OLYMPIC"
120 PRINT "ATHLETE?   I'LL LET YOU FIGURE IT"
130 PRINT "OUT PRECISELY."
140 PRINT
150 PRINT "HOW IS THE RACE MEASURED:"
160 PRINT "METERS, KILOMETERS, YARDS, OR MILES?"
170 INPUT U$
180 T$=MID$(U$,1,2)
190 IF T$="YA" THEN C=.0009144
200 IF T$="MI" THEN C=1.609
210 IF T$="ME" THEN C=.001
220 IF T$="KI" THEN C=1
230 IF T$<>"YA" AND T$<>"MI" AND T$<>"ME" AND T$<>"KI"
    THEN 150
240 PRINT
250 PRINT "HOW MANY ";U$;" IS THE RACE";
260 INPUT D
270 PRINT
280 PRINT "USE COLONS AND DECIMAL POINT"
290 PRINT "TO SEPARATE THE TIME:"
300 PRINT "(3:45:20.2--NOT"
310 PRINT "3 HOURS,45 MINUTES,20.2 SECONDS)"
320 PRINT
330 PRINT "WHAT IS THE ATHLETE'S TIME";
340 INPUT A$
350 IF A$="" THEN 340
360 N=1
370 FOR I=LEN(A$) TO 0 STEP -1
380 IF I=0 THEN 430
390 IF MID$(A$,I,1)<>"." THEN 420
400 N=0
410 GOTO 430
420 IF MID$(A$,I,1)<>":" THEN 500
430 IF N=0 THEN F=VAL(MID$(L$,1,1))
440 IF N=1 THEN S=VAL(L$)
450 IF N=2 THEN M=VAL(L$)
460 IF N=3 THEN H=VAL(L$)
470 N=N+1
480 L$=""
490 GOTO 510
500 L$=MID$(A$,I,1)+L$
510 NEXT I
520 T=H+(M/60)+(S/3600)+(F/36000)
530 PRINT
540 PRINT "THE ATHLETE'S SPEED IS:"
550 PRINT C*D/T; " KILOMETERS PER HOUR"
560 PRINT C*D/T/1.609; " MILES PER HOUR"
```

☐ If You Have . . .

APPLE II

Add: 295 PRINT "TIME MUST BE ENCLOSED IN QUOTES";

ATARI

Add: 95 DIM U$(11),T$(2),A$(11),L$(11)
    465 TX=0
    505 L$(TX)=A$(I,I)

Change: 180 T$=U$(1,2)
    390 IF A$(I,I)<>"." THEN 420
    420 IF A$(I,I)<>":" THEN 500
    430 IF N=0 THEN F=VAL(L$(1,1))
    500 TX=TX+1

COMMODORE 64

Change: 280 PRINT "USE SEMICOLONS AND DECIMAL POINT"
    300 PRINT "(3;45;20.2--NOT"
    420 IF MID$(A$,I,1)<>";" THEN 500

COMMODORE VIC-20

Change: 160 PRINT "METERS, KILOMETERS, YARDS, OR MILES"
    250 PRINT "HOW MANY ";U$;" IS THE RACE"
    280 PRINT "USE SEMICOLONS AND DECIMAL POINT"
    300 PRINT "(3;45;20.2--NOT"
    330 PRINT "WHAT IS THE ATHLETE'S TIME"
    420 IF MID$(A$,I,1)<>";" THEN 500

TEXAS INSTRUMENTS 99/4A

Add: 195 C=.0009144
    205 C=1.609
    215 C=.001
    225 C=1
    435 F=VAL(SEG$(L$,1,1))
    445 S=VAL(L$)
    455 M=VAL(L$)
    465 H=VAL(L$)

Change: 180 T$=SEG$(U$,1,2)
    190 IF T$<>"YA" THEN 200
    200 IF T$<>"MI" THEN 210
    210 IF T$<>"ME" THEN 220
    220 IF T$<>"KI" THEN 230
    230 IF (T$<>"YA")*(T$<>"MI")*(T$<>"ME")*(T$<>"KI")
    THEN 150

(continued)

143

```
390 IF SEG$(A$,I,1)<>"." THEN 420
420 IF SEG$(A$,I,1)<>":" THEN 500
430 IF N<>0 THEN 440
440 IF N<>1 THEN 450
450 IF N<>2 THEN 460
460 IF N<>3 THEN 470
500 L$=SEG$(A$,I,1)&L$
```

TRS-80 COLOR COMPUTER

Change: `340 LINE INPUT A$`

Gold Medal Diver

You're on the high board. Your knees feel weak. Will the judges award
you a high score — or will you end up with no medal at all?
Take the plunge and find out!

☐ Sample Run

```
        O
       -X-
        M
======

YOU ARE ON THE BOARD--
HIT THE ENTER KEY TO MAKE YOUR DIVE?



          W
          X
          O
        I I



             W
             X
             O
           I I



               W
               X
               O
             I I



                 W
                 X
                 O
               I I




                 SPLASH!!
                 SPLASH!!
                 SPLASH!!
                 SPLASH!!
                 SPLASH!!
                 SPLASH!!
                 SPLASH!!


YOUR SCORE WAS 1.1
HOW AWFUL!

WANT TO TRY ANOTHER? NO
```

☐ Program Listing

```
10 REM GOLD MEDAL DIVER
100 K=2
110 PRINT CHR$(12)
120 PRINT TAB(5);"O"
130 PRINT TAB(4);"-X-"
140 PRINT TAB(5);"M"
150 FOR A=1 TO 6
160 PRINT "=";
170 NEXT A
180 PRINT
190 PRINT
200 PRINT "YOU ARE ON THE BOARD--"
210 PRINT "HIT THE ENTER KEY TO MAKE YOUR DIVE";
220 INPUT D$
230 PRINT CHR$(12)
240 IF K=17 THEN 340
250 FOR B=1 TO K
260 PRINT
270 NEXT B
280 PRINT TAB(K);" W "
290 PRINT TAB(K);" X "
300 PRINT TAB(K);" O "
310 PRINT TAB(K);"I I"
320 K=K+1
330 GOTO 230
340 FOR C=1 TO 25
350 PRINT
360 NEXT C
370 FOR D=1 TO 10
380 PRINT TAB(17);"SPLASH!!"
390 NEXT D
400 FOR E=1 TO 25
410 PRINT
420 NEXT E
430 A=INT(RND(1)*9)+1
440 B=INT(RND(1)*9)+1
450 PRINT "YOUR SCORE WAS ";CHR$(48+A);".";CHR$(48+B)
460 ON A GOTO 470,470,490,490,490,490,510,510,510
470 PRINT "HOW AWFUL!"
480 GOTO 520
490 PRINT "JUST AVERAGE!"
500 GOTO 520
510 PRINT "TERRIFIC DIVE!"
520 PRINT
530 PRINT "WANT TO TRY ANOTHER";
540 INPUT D$
550 IF MID$(D$,1,1)<>"N" THEN 100
```

☐ If You Have . . .

APPLE II

Change:
```
110  HOME
210  PRINT "HIT THE RETURN KEY TO MAKE YOUR DIVE"
230  HOME
```

ATARI

Add:
```
 95  DIM D$(3)
565  FOR A=1 TO IDX
575  PRINT " ";:NEXT A:RETURN
```

Change:
```
110  PRINT CHR$(125)
120  IDX=5:GOSUB 565:PRINT "O"
130  IDX=4:GOSUB 565:PRINT "-X-"
140  IDX=5:GOSUB 565:PRINT "M"
210  PRINT "HIT THE RETURN KEY TO MAKE YOUR DIVE";
230  PRINT CHR$(125)
280  IDX=K:GOSUB 565:PRINT " W "
290  GOSUB 565:PRINT " X "
300  GOSUB 565:PRINT " O "
310  GOSUB 565:PRINT "I I"
430  A=INT(RND(0)*9)+1
440  B=INT(RND(0)*9)+1
550  IF D$(1,1)<>"N" THEN 100
```

COMMODORE 64

Change:
```
110  PRINT CHR$(147)
210  PRINT "HIT THE RETURN KEY TO MAKE YOUR DIVE";
230  PRINT CHR$(147)
```

COMMODORE VIC-20

Change:
```
110  PRINT CHR$(147)
210  PRINT "HIT THE RETURN KEY TO MAKE YOUR DIVE"
230  PRINT CHR$(147)
380  PRINT TAB(11);"SPLASH!!"
530  PRINT "WANT TO TRY ANOTHER"
```

TEXAS INSTRUMENTS 99/4A

Add:
```
215  FOR SP=1 TO 16
216  PRINT
217  NEXT SP
315  FOR SP=1 TO 17-K
316  PRINT
317  NEXT SP
```

(continued)

Change:
```
110 CALL CLEAR
230 CALL CLEAR
430 A=INT(RND*9)+1
440 B=INT(RND*9)+1
550 IF SEG$(D$,1,1)<>"N" THEN 100
```

TRS-80 COLOR COMPUTER

Change:
```
110 CLS
230 CLS
340 FOR C=1 TO 15
400 FOR E=1 TO 15
430 A=RND(9)
440 B=RND(9)
```

Steps to Success

The way to win a long race — or a short one — is to put one foot in front of the other, again and again! But how many times do you have to do it?
This is the program that will figure it out!

☐ Sample Run

```
HOW MANY STEPS WILL IT TAKE YOU
TO RUN A RACE?  I'LL FIGURE IT
OUT FOR YOU.

HOW LONG IS YOUR STRIDE,
MEASURED FROM THE HEEL OF
ONE FOOT TO THE OTHER HEEL?

(IN INCHES AND DECIMALS--
NO FRACTIONS, PLEASE)? 11.4

HOW IS THE RACE MEASURED--
YARDS, MILES, METERS, KILOMETERS? METERS

HOW MANY METERS IS THE RACE? 5000

AT A STRIDE OF 11.4 INCHES,
YOU WILL TAKE APPROXIMATELY
17267 STEPS
IN A RACE 5000 METERS LONG.

RUN

HOW MANY STEPS WILL IT TAKE YOU
TO RUN A RACE?  I'LL FIGURE IT
OUT FOR YOU.

HOW LONG IS YOUR STRIDE,
MEASURED FROM THE HEEL OF
ONE FOOT TO THE OTHER HEEL?

(IN INCHES AND DECIMALS--
NO FRACTIONS, PLEASE)? 12.2

HOW IS THE RACE MEASURED--
YARDS, MILES, METERS, KILOMETERS? YARDS

HOW MANY YARDS IS THE RACE? 100

AT A STRIDE OF 12.2 INCHES,
YOU WILL TAKE APPROXIMATELY
295 STEPS
IN A RACE 100 YARDS LONG.
```

□ Program Listing

```
10 REM STEPS TO SUCCESS
100 PRINT
110 PRINT "HOW MANY STEPS WILL IT TAKE YOU"
120 PRINT "TO RUN A RACE?  I'LL FIGURE IT"
130 PRINT "OUT FOR YOU."
140 PRINT
150 PRINT "HOW LONG IS YOUR STRIDE,"
160 PRINT "MEASURED FROM THE HEEL OF"
170 PRINT "ONE FOOT TO THE OTHER HEEL?"
180 PRINT
190 PRINT "(IN INCHES AND DECIMALS--"
200 PRINT "NO FRACTIONS, PLEASE)";
210 INPUT S
220 IF S=0 THEN 190
230 PRINT
240 PRINT "HOW IS THE RACE MEASURED--"
250 PRINT "YARDS, MILES, METERS, KILOMETERS?"
260 INPUT M$
270 L$=MID$(M$,1,2)
280 IF L$="YA" THEN C=36
290 IF L$="MI" THEN C=63360
300 IF L$="ME" THEN C=39.37
310 IF L$="KI" THEN C=39371.9
320 IF L$<>"YA" AND L$<>"MI" AND L$<>"ME" AND L$<>"KI"
    THEN 240
330 PRINT
340 PRINT "HOW MANY ";M$;" IS THE RACE";
350 INPUT N
360 PRINT
370 PRINT "AT A STRIDE OF ";S;" INCHES,"
380 PRINT "YOU WILL TAKE APPROXIMATELY"
390 PRINT INT(N*C/S);" STEPS"
400 PRINT "IN A RACE ";N;" ";M$;" LONG."
410 PRINT
```

☐ If You Have . . .

APPLE II   No Changes Required

ATARI

Add: `95 DIM M$(11),L$(2)`

Change: `270 L$=M$(1,2)`

COMMODORE 64   No Changes Required

COMMODORE VIC-20

Change: `200 PRINT "NO FRACTIONS, PLEASE)"`
`250 PRINT "YARDS, MILES, METERS, KILOMETERS"`
`340 PRINT "HOW MANY ";M$;" IS THE RACE"`

TEXAS INSTRUMENTS 99/4A

Add: `285 C=36`
`295 C=63360`
`305 C=39.37`
`315 C=39371.9`

Change: `270 L$=SEG$(M$,1,2)`
`280 IF L$<>"YA" THEN 290`
`290 IF L$<>"MI" THEN 300`
`300 IF L$<>"ME" THEN 310`
`310 IF L$<>"KI" THEN 320`
`320 IF (L$<>"YA")*(L$<>"MI")*(L$<>"ME")*(L$<>"KI")`
`THEN 240`

TRS-80 COLOR COMPUTER   No Changes Required

Olympic Money

Dollars may make sense to you, but they can be confusing to a foreign visitor. This program will help clear up the mystery. Check a bank or the business section of your newspaper for the current exchange rates.

☐ Sample Run

```
YOU'RE AN ATHLETE VISITING
AMERICA FROM ANOTHER COUNTRY.

YOU WANT TO TAKE SOUVENIRS HOME
BUT YOU NEED TO KNOW THE PRICE
IN YOUR COUNTRY'S MONEY.

WHAT'S THE PRICE IN DOLLARS? 12.50

WHAT'S ONE UNIT OF
YOUR CURRENCY CALLED? SHEKEL

HOW MANY SHEKELS
TO THE DOLLAR? 80

YOU NEED 1000 SHEKELS
TO BUY SOMETHING COSTING
12.50 DOLLARS.

RUN

YOU'RE AN ATHLETE VISITING
AMERICA FROM ANOTHER COUNTRY.

YOU WANT TO TAKE SOUVENIRS HOME
BUT YOU NEED TO KNOW THE PRICE
IN YOUR COUNTRY'S MONEY.

WHAT'S THE PRICE IN DOLLARS? 5.49

WHAT'S ONE UNIT OF
YOUR CURRENCY CALLED? ESCUDO

HOW MANY ESCUDOS
TO THE DOLLAR? 123

YOU NEED 675.27 ESCUDOS
TO BUY SOMETHING COSTING
5.49 DOLLARS.
```

☐ Program Listing

```
10   REM OLYMPIC MONEY
100  PRINT "YOU'RE AN ATHLETE VISITING"
110  PRINT "AMERICA FROM ANOTHER COUNTRY."
120  PRINT
130  PRINT "YOU WANT TO TAKE SOUVENIRS HOME"
140  PRINT "BUT YOU NEED TO KNOW THE PRICE"
150  PRINT "IN YOUR COUNTRY'S MONEY."
160  PRINT
170  PRINT "WHAT'S THE PRICE IN DOLLARS";
180  INPUT C
190  IF C=0 THEN 170
200  PRINT
210  PRINT "WHAT'S ONE UNIT OF"
220  PRINT "YOUR CURRENCY CALLED";
230  INPUT F$
240  IF F$="" THEN 210
250  PRINT
260  PRINT "HOW MANY ";F$;"S"
270  PRINT "TO THE DOLLAR";
280  INPUT D
290  IF D=0 THEN 260
300  PRINT
310  PRINT "YOU NEED ";C*D;" ";F$;"S"
320  PRINT "TO BUY SOMETHING COSTING"
330  PRINT C;" DOLLARS."
340  PRINT
```

☐ If You Have . . .

APPLE II   No Changes Required

ATARI

Add: `95 DIM F$(11)`

COMMODORE 64   No Changes Required

COMMODORE VIC-20

```
Change:  170 PRINT "WHAT'S THE PRICE IN DOLLARS"
         220 PRINT "YOUR CURRENCY CALLED"
         270 PRINT "TO THE DOLLAR"
```

TEXAS INSTRUMENTS 99/4A   No Changes Required

TRS-80 COLOR COMPUTER   No Changes Required

Olympic Medals

By now you've probably won a whole fistful of medals — but you haven't actually seen them. Now it's time for your own personal awards!

☐ Sample Run

```
YOU ARE UP ON THE AWARDS PLATFORM.

YOU HAVE JUST WON AN OLYMPIC EVENT!

     1    GOLD
     2    SILVER
     3    BRONZE

WHICH DID YOU WIN? 3
```

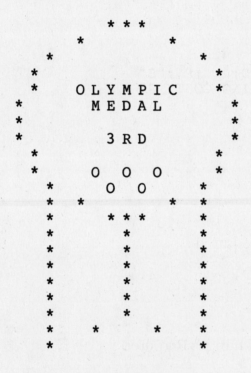

```
     CONGRATULATIONS!!
     WANT TO TRY AGAIN? YES

YOU ARE UP ON THE AWARDS PLATFORM.

YOU HAVE JUST WON AN OLYMPIC EVENT!

     1    GOLD
     2    SILVER
```

```
    3   BRONZE

WHICH DID YOU WIN? 1
```

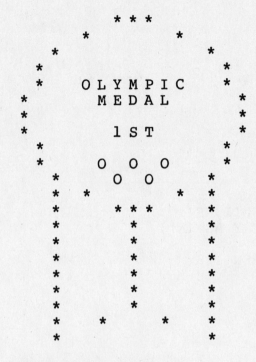

```
CONGRATULATIONS!!
WANT TO TRY AGAIN? NO
```

☐ Program Listing

```
10 REM OLYMPIC MEDALS
100  PRINT CHR$(12)
110  PRINT "YOU ARE UP ON THE AWARDS PLATFORM."
120  PRINT
130  PRINT "YOU HAVE JUST WON AN OLYMPIC EVENT!"
140  PRINT
150  PRINT TAB(5);"1";TAB(10);"GOLD"
160  PRINT TAB(5);"2";TAB(10);"SILVER"
170  PRINT TAB(5);"3";TAB(10);"BRONZE"
180  PRINT
190  PRINT "WHICH DID YOU WIN";
200  INPUT W$
210  IF VAL(W$)<1 OR VAL(W$)>3 THEN 190
220  FOR A=1 TO 20
230  READ A$
240  FOR B=1 TO 17
250  IF VAL(MID$(A$,B,1))>0 THEN 280
260  PRINT MID$(A$,B,1);
270  GOTO 330
```

(continued)

```
280  IF VAL(MID$(A$,B,1))>1 THEN 310
290  PRINT "*";
300  GOTO 330
310  IF ASC(MID$(A$,B,1))>65 THEN 330
320  PRINT CHR$(32);
330  NEXT B
340  PRINT
350  IF A<>7 THEN 420
360  ON VAL(W$) GOTO 370,390,410
370  PRINT "  *        1ST        *"
380  GOTO 420
390  PRINT "  *        2ND        *"
400  GOTO 420
410  PRINT "  *        3RD        *"
420  NEXT A
430  RESTORE
440  PRINT
450  PRINT TAB(3);"CONGRATULATIONS!!"
460  PRINT TAB(3);"WANT TO TRY AGAIN";
470  INPUT Z$
480  IF MID$(Z$,1,1)<>"N" THEN 100
490  END
500  DATA 55555555111777777
510  DATA 44444414444415555
520  DATA 99991999999999166
530  DATA 77717777777777718
540  DATA 2221220LYMPIC2212
550  DATA 3313333MEDAL33331
560  DATA 77177777777777771
570  DATA 66614444444444413
580  DATA 222155505050555515
590  DATA 7777177707O777122
600  DATA 99991919999919166
610  DATA 22221333111222133
620  DATA 44441777713333155
630  DATA 44441777713333155
640  DATA 44441777713333155
650  DATA 44441777713333155
660  DATA 44441777713333155
670  DATA 44441777713333155
680  DATA 22221441333155133
690  DATA 55551666666666177
```

☐ If You Have . . .

APPLE II

Change: 100 HOME

ATARI

```
Add:    95 DIM W$(1),A$(17),Z$(3)
       245 IF ASC(A$(B,B))>64 THEN PRINT A$(B,B);
       246 IF ASC(A$(B,B))>64 THEN 330
       705 FOR A=1 TO IDX
       715 PRINT " ";:NEXT A:RETURN

Change: 100 PRINT CHR$(125)
        150 IDX=5:GOSUB 705:PRINT "1";:GOSUB 705:PRINT
            "GOLD"
        160 GOSUB 705:PRINT "2";:GOSUB 705:PRINT "SILVER"
        170 GOSUB 705:PRINT "3";:GOSUB 705:PRINT "BRONZE"
        250 IF VAL(A$(B,B))>0 THEN 280
        260 PRINT A$(B,B)
        280 IF VAL(A$(B,B))>1 THEN 310
        310 REM
        450 IDX=3:GOSUB 705:PRINT "CONGRATULATIONS!!"
        460 GOSUB 705:PRINT "WANT TO TRY AGAIN";
        480 IF Z$(1,1)<>"N" THEN 100
```

COMMODORE 64

```
Change: 100 PRINT CHR$(147)
```

COMMODORE VIC-20

```
Delete: 640, 650

Change: 100 PRINT CHR$(147)
        190 PRINT "WHICH DID YOU WIN"
        220 FOR A=1 TO 18
        460 PRINT TAB(3);"WANT TO TRY AGAIN"
```

TEXAS INSTRUMENTS 99/4A

```
Add:    245 IF ASC(SEG$(A$,B,1))>64 THEN 310
        315 GOTO 330

Change: 100 CALL CLEAR
        210 IF (VAL(W$)<1)+(VAL(W$)>3) THEN 190
        250 IF VAL(SEG$(A$,B,1))>0 THEN 280
        260 PRINT SEG$(A$,B,1);
        280 IF VAL(SEG$(A$,B,1))>1 THEN 320
        310 PRINT SEG$(A$,B,1);
        480 IF SEG$(Z$,1,1)<>"N" THEN 100
```

TRS-80 COLOR COMPUTER

```
Change: 100 CLS
```

Olympic Wrestler

Are you a paperweight? Even if you're a human being, the answer could well be yes. Grapple with this program, and you'll find out exactly where you belong in the world of Olympic wrestling.

☐ Sample Run

```
WHAT KIND OF WRESTLER ARE YOU?
STEP ON THE SCALES, PLEASE!

HOW MANY POUNDS DO YOU WEIGH? 113

YOU WEIGH 51.24716 KILOGRAMS.

YOU WEIGH MORE THAN 105 POUNDS
(48 KILOGRAMS)
BUT NOT MORE THAN 114 POUNDS
(52 KILOGRAMS).
YOU ARE A FLYWEIGHT WRESTLER.

RUN

WHAT KIND OF WRESTLER ARE YOU?
STEP ON THE SCALES, PLEASE!

HOW MANY POUNDS DO YOU WEIGH? 222


YOU WEIGH MORE THAN 220 POUNDS
(100 KILOGRAMS).
YOU ARE A SUPER-HEAVYWEIGHT WRESTLER.
```

☐ Program Listing

```
10 REM OLYMPIC WRESTLER
100 PRINT
110 PRINT "WHAT KIND OF WRESTLER ARE YOU?"
120 PRINT "STEP ON THE SCALES, PLEASE!"
130 PRINT
140 PRINT "HOW MANY POUNDS DO YOU WEIGH";
150 INPUT W
160 IF W=0 THEN 140
170 PRINT
180 IF W>220 THEN 280
190 READ T
200 IF T=81 THEN 240
```

```
210 IF W<=T*2.205 THEN 240
220 M=T
230 GOTO 190
240 FOR I=1 TO 9
250 READ C$
260 NEXT I
270 GOTO 320
280 PRINT "YOU WEIGH MORE THAN 220 POUNDS."
290 PRINT "(100 KILOGRAMS)"
300 PRINT "YOU ARE A SUPER-HEAVYWEIGHT WRESTLER."
310 END
320 PRINT "YOU WEIGH ";W/2.205;" KILOGRAMS."
330 PRINT
340 PRINT "YOU WEIGH MORE THAN ";INT(M*2.205);" POUNDS"
350 PRINT "(";M;" KILOGRAMS)"
360 PRINT "BUT NOT MORE THAN ";INT(T*2.205);" POUNDS"
370 PRINT "(";T;" KILOGRAMS)."
380 PRINT "YOU ARE A ";C$;"WEIGHT WRESTLER."
390 DATA 48,52,57,62,68
400 DATA 74,82,90,100
410 DATA PAPER,FLY
420 DATA BANTAM,FEATHER
430 DATA LIGHT,WELTER,MIDDLE
440 DATA LIGHT HEAVY,HEAVY
```

☐ If You Have . . .

APPLE II   No Changes Required

ATARI

Add: `95 DIM C$(11)`

COMMODORE 64   No Changes Required

COMMODORE VIC-20

Change: `140 PRINT "HOW MANY POUNDS DO YOU WEIGH"`

TEXAS INSTRUMENTS 99/4A   No Changes Required

TRS-80 COLOR COMPUTER   No Changes Required

Basketball Action

Your team is playing the very last seconds of the final Olympic basketball
game. Either side can win — but there's not much time left!
Remember: just as on the court, the farther you are from the basket, the
harder it is to make your shot. And don't forget
that this is a game of teamwork.
Put on your basketball shoes, and dribble away!

☐ Sample Run

```
ENTER YOUR LAST NAME? DILLON
ENTER THE LAST NAME OF A FRIEND? SPERBER
THE LAST NAME OF ANOTHER FRIEND? MARTIN
THE LAST NAME OF ANOTHER FRIEND? CROWLEY
THE LAST NAME OF ANOTHER FRIEND? MARTINEZ

THE SCORE IS TIED:
HOW MANY POINTS DOES EACH TEAM HAVE? 84

YOU'RE ON THE OLYMPIC
BASKETBALL TEAM.  THE FINAL GAME
IS TIED WITH JUST 30 SECONDS
LEFT TO PLAY.

YOUR TEAMMATES ARE:
SPERBER
MARTIN
CROWLEY
MARTINEZ

YOU'RE 7 FEET FROM THE BASKET.
WHAT DO YOU DO NOW?
1: PASS
2: SHOOT
3: DRIVE TOWARD THE BASKET

QUICK! WHAT'S YOUR CHOICE? 1

WHO WILL YOU PASS TO? MARTIN
MARTIN HAS THE BALL!
MARTIN SHOOTS!
THE BALL RIMS THE BASKET
AND GOES IN!
TWO POINTS!

THERE ARE 24 SECONDS LEFT.
HIT THE ENTER KEY TO CONTINUE?

THE OPPOSING FORWARD HAS THE BALL.
```

AND MOVES DOWNCOURT.
THE OPPOSING FORWARD SHOOTS!
SWISH!
TWO POINTS!

THERE ARE 14 SECONDS LEFT.
HIT THE ENTER KEY TO CONTINUE?

DILLON HAS THE BALL.
AND MOVES DOWNCOURT.
YOU'RE 5 FEET FROM THE BASKET.
WHAT DO YOU DO NOW?
1: PASS
2: SHOOT
3: DRIVE TOWARD THE BASKET

QUICK! WHAT'S YOUR CHOICE? 2

DILLON SHOOTS!
THE BALL RIMS THE BASKET
AND GOES IN!
TWO POINTS!

THERE ARE 4 SECONDS LEFT.
HIT THE ENTER KEY TO CONTINUE?

THE OPPOSING FORWARD HAS THE BALL.
AND MOVES DOWNCOURT.
THE OPPOSING FORWARD DRIVES TOWARD THE BASKET.
TWO DEFENDERS BLOCK THE WAY
AT 2 FEET FROM THE BASKET.

THE BUZZER SOUNDS!
THE GAME IS OVER!
YOUR TEAM WINS THE GOLD MEDAL!

☐ Program Listing

```
10 REM BASKETBALL ACTION
100 TF$="THE OPPOSING FORWARD"
110 PRINT "ENTER YOUR LAST NAME:"
120 INPUT Y$
130 IF Y$="" THEN 110
140 B$=Y$
150 FOR I=1 TO 4
160 IF I=1 THEN PRINT "ENTER THE LAST NAME OF A FRIEND:"
170 IF I<>1 THEN PRINT "THE LAST NAME OF ANOTHER FRIEND:"
180 IF I=1 THEN INPUT F1$
190 IF F1$="" THEN 160
200 IF I=2 THEN INPUT F2$
210 IF I>1 AND F2$="" THEN 170
220 IF I=3 THEN INPUT F3$
```

(continued)

```
230 IF I>2 AND F3$="" THEN 170
240 IF I=4 THEN INPUT F4$
250 IF I>3 AND F4$="" THEN 170
260 NEXT I
270 PRINT
280 PRINT "THE SCORE IS TIED:"
290 PRINT "HOW MANY POINTS DOES EACH TEAM HAVE?"
300 INPUT P
310 IF P=0 THEN 290
320 RANDOMIZE P
330 PRINT
340 S=20+INT(RND(1)*30)
350 PRINT "YOU'RE ON THE OLYMPIC"
360 PRINT "BASKETBALL TEAM.  THE FINAL GAME"
370 PRINT "IS TIED WITH JUST ";S; " SECONDS"
380 PRINT "LEFT TO PLAY."
390 PRINT
400 PRINT "YOUR TEAMMATES ARE:"
410 PRINT F1$
420 PRINT F2$
430 PRINT F3$
440 PRINT F4$
450 PRINT
460 J=INT(RND(1)*25)+1
470 PRINT "YOU'RE ";J;" FEET FROM THE BASKET."
480 PRINT "WHAT DO YOU DO NOW?"
490 PRINT "1: PASS"
500 PRINT "2: SHOOT"
510 PRINT "3: DRIVE TOWARD THE BASKET"
520 PRINT
530 PRINT "QUICK! WHAT'S YOUR CHOICE";
540 INPUT C
550 PRINT
560 IF C<1 OR C>3 THEN 480
570 IF C=1 THEN 600
580 IF C=2 THEN 980
590 IF C=3 THEN 1180
600 REM ------PASS SUBROUTINE-------
610 PRINT "WHO WILL YOU PASS TO";
620 INPUT P$
630 IF P$="" THEN 610
640 FOR I=1 TO 4
650 IF P$=F1$ THEN B$=F1$
660 IF P$=F2$ THEN B$=F2$
670 IF P$=F3$ THEN B$=F3$
680 IF P$=F4$ THEN B$=F4$
690 IF P$<>F1$ AND P$<>F2$ AND P$<>F3$ AND P$<>F4$ THEN 760
700 NEXT I
710 IF 1+INT(RND(1)*10)<3 THEN 740
720 PRINT B$;" HAS THE BALL!"
730 GOTO 890
740 PRINT B$;" MISSES THE BALL!"
750 GOTO 780
760 PRINT "NO TEAMMATE BY THAT NAME!"
770 PRINT "YOU THROW THE BALL AWAY!"
```

```
780  S=S-1
790  GOTO 1330
800  REM -----TIME SUBROUTINE--------
810  S=S-1
820  IF S<1 THEN 1660
830  PRINT
840  PRINT "THERE ARE ";S;" SECONDS LEFT."
850  PRINT "HIT THE ENTER KEY TO CONTINUE";
860  INPUT X$
870  PRINT
880  RETURN
890  REM ---TEAMMATE'S BALL SUBROUTINE---
900  J=J-(INT(RND(1)*J))
910  IF 1+INT(RND(1)*10)<5 THEN 930
920  GOTO 980
930  PRINT B$;" PASSES TO ";Y$
940  B$=Y$
950  J=J-(INT(RND(1)*J))
960  GOSUB 800
970  GOTO 470
980  REM ------SHOOT SUBROUTINE--------
990  PRINT B$;" SHOOTS!"
1000 IF 1+INT(RND(1)*25)<J THEN 1120
1010 IF INT(RND(1)*2)<1 THEN 1050
1020 PRINT "THE BALL RIMS THE BASKET"
1030 PRINT "AND GOES IN!"
1040 GOTO 1060
1050 PRINT "SWISH!"
1060 PRINT "TWO POINTS!"
1070 IF B$<>TF$ THEN YP=YP+2
1080 IF B$=TF$ THEN TP=TP+2
1090 S=S-5
1100 GOSUB 800
1110 GOTO 1330
1120 PRINT "THE BALL BOUNCES OFF THE BACKBOARD"
1130 PRINT "AND RIMS THE BASKET"
1140 PRINT "BUT BOUNCES AWAY!"
1150 S=S+2
1160 GOSUB 800
1170 GOTO 1330
1180 REM ------DRIBBLE SUBROUTINE---------
1190 IF DRIB<1 THEN 1210
1200 IF INT(RND(1)*10)<5 THEN 1260
1210 PRINT B$;" DRIVES TOWARD THE BASKET."
1220 PRINT "TWO DEFENDERS BLOCK THE WAY"
1230 J=J-INT(RND(1)*J)
1240 PRINT "AT ";J;" FEET FROM THE BASKET."
1250 GOSUB 800
1260 IF INT(RND(1)*10)<2 THEN 1460
1270 IF INT(RND(1)*10)>4 THEN 1310
1280 PRINT "A STEAL!"
1290 DRIB=0
1300 GOTO 1330
1310 IF B$=Y$ THEN 470
1320 ON 1+INT(RND(1)*3) GOTO 980,1180,1460
```

(continued)

```
1330  REM -------OPPONENTS' BALL-------
1340  IF B$<>TF$ THEN 1370
1350  B$=Y$
1360  GOTO 1380
1370  B$=TF$
1380  PRINT
1390  PRINT B$;" HAS THE BALL."
1400  PRINT "AND MOVES DOWNCOURT."
1410  S=S-4
1420  J=INT(RND(1)*25)+1
1430  IF B$<>Y$ AND INT(RND(1)*10)<5 THEN 980
1440  IF B$<>Y$ THEN 1180
1450  GOTO 470
1460  REM -----FOUL SUBROUTINE--------
1470  PRINT "FOUL!"
1480  PRINT
1490  PRINT B$;" GETS TWO FOUL SHOTS!"
1500  PRINT "SHOT NUMBER";F+1;". . . "
1510  PRINT
1520  PRINT "HIT THE ENTER KEY FOR THE SHOT";
1530  INPUT X$
1540  IF INT(RND(1)*10)<8 THEN 1580
1550  PRINT "MISSED!"
1560  F=F+1
1570  GOTO 1620
1580  PRINT "MADE IT!"
1590  IF B$=TF$ THEN TP=TP+1
1600  IF B$<>TF$ THEN YP=YP+1
1610  F=F+1
1620  GOSUB 800
1630  IF F=1 THEN 1500
1640  F=0
1650  GOTO 1330
1660  PRINT
1670  PRINT "THE BUZZER SOUNDS!"
1680  PRINT "THE GAME IS OVER!"
1690  IF YP>TP THEN 1740
1700  IF YP=TP THEN 1760
1710  PRINT "YOUR TEAM LOSES THE FINAL GAME!"
1720  PRINT "YOU'LL HAVE TO SETTLE FOR SILVER."
1730  END
1740  PRINT "YOUR TEAM WINS THE GOLD MEDAL!"
1750  END
1760  PRINT "IT'S A TIE--"
1770  PRINT "PLAY A TIEBREAKER TO SEE WHO WINS!"
```

☐ If You Have . . .

APPLE II

Delete: 320

Change: 850 PRINT "HIT THE RETURN KEY TO CONTINUE";
1520 PRINT "HIT THE RETURN KEY FOR THE SHOT";

ATARI

Delete: 320

Add: 92   DIM Y$(14),P$(14),B$(20),F1$(14),F2$(14),
F3$(14),F4$(14)
94   DIM TF$(20),X$(1)

Change: 340 S=20+INT(RND(0)*30)
460 J=INT(RND(0)*25)+1
710 IF 1+INT(RND(0)*10)<3 THEN 740
850 PRINT "HIT THE RETURN KEY TO CONTINUE";
900 J=J-(INT(RND(0)*J))
910 IF 1+INT(RND(0)*10)<5 THEN 930
950 J=J-(INT(RND(0)*J))
1000 IF 1+INT(RND(0)*25)<J THEN 1120
1010 IF INT(RND(0)*2)<1 THEN 1050
1200 IF INT(RND(0)*10)<5 THEN 1260
1230 J=J-INT(RND(0)*J)
1260 IF INT(RND(0)*10)<2 THEN 1460
1270 IF INT(RND(0)*10)>4 THEN 1310
1320 ON 1+INT(RND(0)*3) GOTO 980,1180,1460
1420 J=INT(RND(0)*25)+1
1430 IF B$<>Y$ AND INT(RND(0)*10)<5 THEN 980
1520 PRINT "HIT THE RETURN KEY FOR THE SHOT";
1540 IF INT(RND(0)*10)<8 THEN 1580

COMMODORE 64

Delete: 320

Change: 340 S=20+INT(RND(0)*30)
460 J=INT(RND(0)*25)+1
710 IF 1+INT(RND(0)*10)<3 THEN 740
850 PRINT "HIT THE RETURN KEY TO CONTINUE";
900 J=J-(INT(RND(0)*J))
910 IF 1+INT(RND(0)*10)<5 THEN 930
950 J=J-(INT(RND(0)*J))
1000 IF 1+INT(RND(0)*25)<J THEN 1120
1010 IF INT(RND(0)*2)<1 THEN 1050
1200 IF INT(RND(0)*10)<5 THEN 1260
1230 J=J-INT(RND(0)*J)
1260 IF INT(RND(0)*10)<2 THEN 1460

(continued)

```
1270 IF INT(RND(Ø)*1Ø)>4 THEN 1310
1320 ON 1+INT(RND(Ø)*3) GOTO 980,1180,1460
1420 J=INT(RND(Ø)*25)+1
1430 IF B$<>Y$ AND INT(RND(Ø)*10)<5 THEN 980
1520 PRINT "HIT THE RETURN KEY FOR THE SHOT";
1540 IF INT(RND(Ø)*1Ø)<8 THEN 1580
```

COMMODORE VIC-20

Delete: 270,320,330,390,450,550,600,800,830,870,890,980,
          1180,1330,1380,1460,1480,1510,1660

Change:
```
340 S=20+INT(RND(Ø)*30)
460 J=INT(RND(Ø)*25)+1
530 PRINT "QUICK! WHAT'S YOUR CHOICE"
570 IF C=1 THEN 610
580 IF C=2 THEN 990
590 IF C=3 THEN 1190
610 PRINT "WHO WILL YOU PASS TO"
710 IF 1+INT(RND(Ø)*1Ø)<3 THEN 740
730 GOTO 900
790 GOTO 1340
820 IF S<1 THEN 1670
850 PRINT "HIT THE RETURN KEY TO CONTINUE"
900 J=J-(INT(RND(Ø)*J))
910 IF 1+INT(RND(Ø)*1Ø)<5 THEN 930
920 GOTO 990
950 J=J-(INT(RND(Ø)*J))
960 GOSUB 810
1000 IF 1+INT(RND(Ø)*25)<J THEN 1120
1010 IF INT(RND(Ø)*2)<1 THEN 1050
1100 GOSUB 810
1110 GOTO 1340
1160 GOSUB 810
1170 GOTO 1340
1200 IF INT(RND(Ø)*1Ø)<5 THEN 1260
1230 J=J-INT(RND(Ø)*J)
1250 GOSUB 810
1260 IF INT(RND(Ø)*1Ø)<2 THEN 1470
1270 IF INT(RND(Ø)*1Ø)<4 THEN 1310
1300 GOTO 1340
1320 ON 1+INT(RND(Ø)*3) GOTO 990,1190,1470
1360 GOTO 1390
1420 J=INT(RND(Ø)*25)+1
1430 IF B$<>Y$ AND INT(RND(1)*1Ø)<5 THEN 990
1440 IF B$<>Y$ THEN 1190
1520 PRINT "HIT THE RETURN KEY FOR THE SHOT"
1540 IF INT(RND(Ø)*1Ø)<8 THEN 1580
1620 GOSUB 810
1650 GOTO 1340
```

TEXAS INSTRUMENTS 99/4A

```
Add:    165 PRINT "ENTER THE LAST NAME OF A FRIEND"
        166 GOTO 180
        185 INPUT F1$
        195 GOTO 260
        215 GOTO 260
        235 GOTO 260
        655 B$=F1$
        665 B$=F2$
        675 B$=F3$
        685 B$=F4$
       1083 GOTO 1090
       1085 YP=YP+2
       1601 GOTO 1610
       1605 TP=TP+1

Change: 160 IF I<>1 THEN 170
        170 PRINT "ENTER THE LAST NAME OF ANOTHER FRIEND"
        180 ON I GOTO 185,200,220,240
        200 INPUT F2$
        210 IF F2$="" THEN 170
        220 INPUT F3$
        230 IF F3$="" THEN 170
        240 INPUT F4$
        250 IF F4$="" THEN 170
        340 S=20+INT(RND*30)
        460 J=INT(RND*25)+1
        560 IF (C<1)+(C>3) THEN 480
        650 IF P$<>F1$ THEN 660
        660 IF P$<>F2$ THEN 670
        670 IF P$<>F3$ THEN 680
        680 IF P$<>F4$ THEN 690
        690 IF (P$<>F1$)*(P$<>F2$)*(P$<>F3$)*(P$<>F4$)
            THEN 760
        710 IF 1+INT(RND*10)<3 THEN 740
        900 J=J-(INT(RND*J))
        910 IF 1+INT(RND*10)<5 THEN 930
        950 J=J-(INT(RND*J))
       1000 IF INT(RND*25)<J THEN 1120
       1010 IF INT(RND*2)<1 THEN 1050
       1070 IF B$<>TF$ THEN 1085
       1080 TP=TP+2
       1200 IF INT(RND*10)<5 THEN 1260
       1230 J=J-INT(RND*J)
       1260 IF INT(RND*10)<2 THEN 1460
       1270 IF INT(RND*10)>4 THEN 1310
       1320 ON 1+INT(RND*3) GOTO 980,1180,1460
       1420 J=INT(RND*25)+1
       1430 IF (B$<>Y$)*(INT(RND*10)<5) THEN 980
       1540 IF INT(RND*10)<8 THEN 1580
       1590 IF B$=TF$ THEN 1605
       1600 YP=YP+1
```

TRS-80 COLOR COMPUTER

Delete: 320,330,390,520

Change:

```
340  S=19+RND(30)
360  PRINT "BASKETBALL TEAM.  THE FINAL GAME";
460  J=RND(25)
710  IF RND(10)<3 THEN 740
900  IF J<3 THEN J=1 ELSE J=J-RND(J)+1
910  IF RND(10)<5 THEN 930
950  IF J<3 THEN J=1 ELSE J=J-RND(J)+1
1000 IF RND(25)<J THEN 1120
1010 IF RND(2)<2 THEN 1050
1200 IF RND(10)-1<5 THEN 1260
1230 IF J<3 THEN J=1 ELSE J=J-RND(J)+1
1260 IF RND(10)-1<2 THEN 1460
1270 IF RND(10)-1>4 THEN 1310
1320 ON RND(3) GOTO 980,1180,1460
1420 J=RND(25)
1430 IF B$<>Y$ AND RND(10)-1<5 THEN 980
1540 IF RND(10)-1<8 THEN 1580
```

MORE FUN! LESS TYPING!

If you just finished typing in all the programs in this book and your pet gerbil ate the disk or cassette you saved them on...

If you're already enjoying the shorter programs in this book, but your fingers tremble at the thought of typing in the longer ones...

If your secretary does all your typing, but she's on a year-long vacation in Moose Jaw, Saskatchewan...

Or if you'd just like to have all these programs handy on a disk or cassette that'll run on your machine...

You're in luck!

You can get every single program in this book (along with extra bonus programs not included in this book) on ready-to-run cassettes or disks, for only $19.95 per book. You can also get tapes or disks for any of the *other* exciting books in this series.

(As a special bonus, order any three, and we'll throw in the fourth one *absolutely free*—so you can enjoy the entire set—and we'll pay all postage and handling!)

Programs are available in one format only (disk *or* cassette) for each specific computer, so please make sure you have the proper equipment before ordering. Remember to check off BOTH the set of programs you want AND the type of machine you have.

Hard/Soft Inc., PO Box 1277, Riverdale, NY 10471

Yes! Please send me the ready-to-run programs I've checked off below.

1. **Check off which format you want:**
- ☐ ATARI cassette tapes
- ☐ APPLE II/II PLUS/IIE disks
- ☐ COMMODORE 64 disks
- ☐ COMMODORE VIC-20 disks
- ☐ IBM PC/PCjr disks
- ☐ TEXAS INSTRUMENTS 99/4A cassette tapes
- ☐ TRS-80 COLOR COMPUTER cassette tapes

2. **Check off which programs you are ordering:**
- ☐ Computer Craziness ($19.95)
- ☐ Computer Monsters ($19.95)
- ☐ Computer Olympics ($19.95)
- ☐ Computer Space Adventures ($19.95)
- ☐ ALL FOUR BOOKS (SPECIAL PRICE $59.85)

3. **PRINT your name and address, and fill in the amount you are enclosing: (Add applicable sales taxes!)**

I am enclosing $19.95 PLUS $2.00 postage and handling and applicable sales tax for each. Total: $_____

☐ *SPECIAL BONUS: Check this box, enclose $59.85, and we'll send you all FOUR sets of programs for the price of three—and we'll pay all postage! This is a savings of over $20.00.*

PRINT your name _____

PRINT your address _____

City _____ *State* _____ *Zip* _____

Make checks payable to Hard/Soft, Inc. Allow 2–8 weeks for delivery.